A Cry In the Wilderness

Gregory R Reid

ISBN-13: 978-1466406728

DEDICATION

To those who have faithfully supported the ministry the Lord has given me all these years – thank you for helping me carry out this calling with courage and confidence. Your letters and notes of encouragement have all been kept in a "book of remembrance" to re-read when the days are not easy, when heaven seems far, and the road becomes a little blurry. Your prayers and love have given me clarity, fortitude and a glimpse of the glory just around the bend.

CONTENTS

FOREWORD

These articles were written over the course of about 12 years. Although many of them were written about things that were taking place in the church and in the world at the time, they remain important and extremely relevant to the challenges we are facing today – perhaps more so as we approach the coming of the Lord. May they challenge you to the core of your commitment, and encourage you to fight on steady till dawn.

Gregory R Reid

1 DENYING THE DEVIL

There are some Christians who are obsessed with the devil. Their lives are wrapped up in what he's doing – not in what Jesus did. But frankly, they are in the minority. Most Christians I know don't give Satan a second thought. In fact, according to a Barna poll, the majority of people in the US who call themselves Christians do not believe in the devil or the Holy Spirit. It is to that I must speak.

I came to know Jesus by direct revelation. I was delivered from the world of the occult and demons because Jesus Himself appeared to me – or rather, He took me to Himself in heaven. I do not say that lightly – it is the absolute truth before God.

My battle to be free of demons was real. The confrontation to demand my full release was not a fantasy. And since that time nearly 32 years ago, that battle has continued in the lives God has brought to me to help deliver from their evil grip. They have made it clear, both in invisible action and visible confrontation, that if they could destroy me utterly, they would. They have tried, and only by God's mercy, they have failed. But the battle has never ceased.

The Holy Spirit is a real Person. He has comforted and instructed me from the beginning. I dare not engage satanic forces without Jesus' authority or the power of the Holy Spirit. After all, Jesus cast out demons – and commanded us to do the same.

We stand on the cusp of one of the greatest outpourings of demonic forces in history. And where does the church stand in this country? If the statistics are our indicator, then it appears we are powerless, denying that demons and the devil are even real – or if they are, so what? Just accentuate the positive.

Why should we be concerned? Because the occult is permeating everything around us: TV, movies, music, games, and education. Now, if you don't believe in the Bible, or just the portions you like, you can stop reading now.

But if you do believe in the whole Bible as God's Word, then you understand that not only is all occult practice (little or big) forbidden, but also that the occult world is owned by demonic spirits, and that practicing the occult results in oppression and often demonization. That means that an increasing number of kids and adults who come to church have this influence. And we aren't prepared to deal with it. Frankly, we don't know how.

I have been fishing around the Internet lately in Christian "apologetic" groups. Many seem to be made up of the same "like-minded" people who deny the dangers of the occult, the same ones who have labored so diligently to silence the voices of those who sound the warning cry. Many of these people are the same ones who have, in effect, wiped out the playing field. With the exception of perhaps Neil Anderson, author of the Bondage Breakers, and a handful of tiny ministries, the standard that opposed occultism and its influence has been taken down and shredded. Call it a preemptive strike to ensure the church is powerless and helpless against what is coming. The subsequent acceptance – or at least winking at – occult books like Twilight and Harry Potter, and acceptance of Christianized Yoga and sanitized Wiccan-like "circle making" prayer methods – have allowed the enemy to slowly pollute the stream of the church with foul occult waters.

I am not suggesting we should obsess over the devil. I certainly don't. But ignore his plan at your own peril. (1 Peter 5:8)

It was common for the New Testament church and leaders to be confronted with demons and the occult. (Acts 8:18-24, Acts 14; 11-14, acts 16:16-18, etc.) Jesus said this would be part of our work. (Mark 16:17-18). If you truly live a Spirit-filled life, you will confront this. And if you minister to broken, addicted people, this may also be part of it.

Instead of equipping and preparing believers to do so, the new wave of Christian intellectuals and apologetic elitists are not only downplaying – sometimes even denying – the existence of the demonic kingdom, they are determined to minimize, criticize and dismiss anyone or anything that promotes the need for "spiritual warfare."

If our battle, as Paul said, is not against flesh and blood, but against powers, principalities and spiritual wickedness in high places, (Eph. 6:12) then the war is not against philosophies, principles, and secular worldviews in high places. We are fighting an intelligent, invisible army. Even the Archangel Michael contended with their warlords. (Daniel 10:13) These real demons and princes of hell did not go away in the New Testament. They are firmly entrenched against us NOW.

And the tragedy is, their strategy has been to get believers to ignore them, deny their existence, dismiss their weapons and compromise our congregations with occultic cancers. We have surrendered more territory than you can imagine. That's why Wicca is one of the fastest growing religion among youth: We have denied the seriousness of both occult powers and the need for God's power in our lives, and the inherent recognition of the supernatural as real and needed by youth and in youth was dismissed – and a whole generation of kids began following the only options left to them – the occult, witchcraft and satanic practices – or just yielding to atheism, in the absence of any discernible power of God in most churches.

In denying the reality of the devil and ignoring him, we've played into his hands perfectly. Because the devil, if you ignore him, will be as quiet as a church mouse. He won't disturb your peace as long as you don't disturb him. But if you once shine the light of truth on our compromises, you will see him as plain as day – and you will have his full attention. And you had better be armored to fight when you do.

Demonic armies are like spiritual "sleeper cells"- they are among us – hidden in our compromises, our false security and our powerless Christian walks. They avoid obvious "September 11" type strikes. All their poison is coated in honey. And they ridicule, along with those Christian intellectual elitists, anyone who says they are real, or try to expose them. We're our own Tokyo Rose.

So what do we do? We must wake up adults and equip our youth and children. The greatest preparation we can give our kids is the Power of God and His Anointing to storm hell's gates. We must teach them "not to be ignorant of Satan's devices". We must give them basic boot camp on the enemy's ways. Then we must make them recognize the war for the lost and bound – that we are not called to be comfortable and happy, but each is called to the fight to redeem the lost.

We must make them know their purpose, and the Power of God to fulfill it. We must make them proactive, reactive, and scrappy little soldiers ready and willing to take the world on for Jesus and to defeat the "sleeper cells" of spiritual compromise in our midst and in the world.

We have a long way to go. To fail to try is to insure our defeat by default, and we will remain an emasculated and irrelevant social club rather than the mighty army God has called us to be.

2 HALF A BOOK: OR, TERRIFIED BY TORAH

When was the last time you heard a message preached out of the Old Testament? My guess is, probably not in a while.

Why is that?

During Easter, there were a number of TV specials on the life of Jesus, some really bad, a few that were passable. But one struck some chords, as they detailed how the message of Jesus was systematically removed from its Jewish foundations over the years.

Most of today's churches have been completely sanitized from any trace of Jewishness. Jesus may as well have been from the moon as from the tribe of David.

Paul spoke profoundly when He said, "I did not fail to declare to you the whole counsel of God." (Acts 20:27)

As a new believer, I read the scriptures like a starving man, tattering my Bible by underlining everything I read in one year. I never saw it as two books, and I rarely just had a New Testament. It was one book to me – The Word of the Lord. The whole of it is about one God, and one Messiah. The Torah, the "Old Testament" is full of Jesus, and the "New Testament" is intricately and inseparably woven with the Old.

My concern is that most Christians – and most pulpits – have a real aversion to the "Old Testament". We like the Psalms, the Song of Solomon is good for marriage week, and the Proverbs seem to be practical enough to extract one or two occasionally. But Ezra? Ezekiel? Habakuk? We rarely go there!

Why is that?

First, I think the "Old Testament" scares us. "The God of the Old

Testament" scares us! Doesn't He? So, many have partitioned God into the God of the Old Testament, and then Jesus. We like Jesus, at least our Westernized version – soft, flowing blond hair, blue eyes, looking beatific and harmless, always suffering, always forgiving. It's one of the things that irks me about some of the comments from new wave "emergent" Christians about the message and life of Jesus – "It's about love, peace, brotherhood and forgiveness!" No, it is NOT. Jesus was about an eternal rescue mission from sin and hell at the cost of His own blood! It was love that was given in the face of CRUCIFIXION. It was peace only obtained by Christ's tearing down the wall of separation between us and God through His sacrifice. It is forgiveness extended from a bloody cross to those who would repent and return!

I realize most people prefer the Jesus that most resembles a hippie who does everything but say, "Why can't we just get along?" We can all pick things we like about Jesus and what He said. But we also ignore and exclude the things that make us squirm. When I hear some people in sermons describing Jesus in flowery, weepy sermons, I want to scream, "What Bible are YOU reading?!?" Yes, He WAS kind, loving and compassionate. But to the religious and proud He was harsh. In anger He upturned the tables of the merchants in the Temple. He cursed a fig tree to death. He makes me tremble! He is the One with Fire in His Eyes, and words like thunder that made John, the very one that lay his head on Jesus' breast, fall on his face like a dead man. (I'm thankful Jesus then touched him and said, "Don't be afraid, John. It's Me.") But no one can read the Gospels and the rest of the New Testament without understanding that Jesus is NOT our personal fluffy-bunny.

We talk of the God of the Old Testament as if He was a different person than He is now. Yet He says, "I am the Lord God, I do not change."

Some things Jesus said are far harsher than anything I've read in the Old Testament. And believers are missing more than they can imagine by not plumbing the depths of the Old for the true character of our Father and our God. He is a father who compassionately loves His children (Psalm 103:13). He's a Father who can't bear to be without us or to forget us (Isaiah 49:15) and a God who cares not just for people but for even cattle. (Jonah 4:11) He is a Father who cared for a little crippled boy named Mephibosheth and took him from poverty and exile and set him at the King's table.

Until you make the "Old Testament" a whole with the New, until you read it and study it diligently with the New, you will never get the complete picture. Most of the New Testament makes little sense to me without the understanding that the Old gives. How in the world can you make any sense of Revelation until you understand its companion, Daniel?

I could continue much more but for now I just wanted to provoke you a little: Why are we afraid of the Old Testament? I think it is partially because when we begin to pursue its study, not just in little pieces we like but in whole, we have to throw up our hands at some point and admit we know NEXT TO NOTHING about God! And that is GOOD! How arrogant of us to think we could distill him into little bite-size sermons and teachings and make people feel like we've got it! He is greater and deeper than we can ever imagine. We KNOW Him because of Jesus, as a friend, Father and companion. But it will take eternity to know Him, and we can only begin by admitting how very small our understanding is. And nothing does that for me like a good dose of the Torah. (Old Testament.) With that humility I am then led to admit that everything I've read about Jesus in the New is just a tiny fragment of what is to be known of Him. I am not afraid anymore – the One Book has become an amazing adventure to me!

The "God of the Old Testament" is the same as the New. Jesus is the express image of all that God is. "If you have seen Me, you have seen the Father." (John 14:9) Embrace the Torah – the Old – the Prophets and the Songs just as you would Paul's letters and the Gospels. Only as you embrace it all is One Book can you truly become a workman who need not be ashamed, ready for any work and any mission God calls you to do.

3 TRUTH TELLERS

"The truth will bring the world's wrath on those who dare to speak it."

Consider this message a warning.

This word came to me unexpectedly one Sunday recently in church. It was neither on my mind nor part of the message. It chilled me.

We are at a crossroads in our nation The decisions we as believers make in this our are not about democrat and republican, but about our hearts, about our future.

I honestly do not know, save for God's grace, why judgment has not yet come to us. It is sheer arrogance among believers to think it's because we're sending so many missionaries around the world. (We are in fact wasting most of our resources on US.) As if God could not raise up missionaries out of stones! Perhaps only prayer for mercy has stayed his hand, the prayer of Abraham: "Lord, will you spare Sodom for one righteous?" Perhaps.

The prophetic edge of my heart has grown sharper the last few years. For reasons I did not understand, when the election in 2000 was thrown to the Supreme Court, I somehow knew God had intervened. Then came September 11.

For a brief shining, tragic moment, our nation came together as one. But from the very moment we were attacked, I knew: "They will soon forget. THEY WILL FORGET!" And so we have. For one moment, the nation prayed. But we have forgotten why. Soon, it was business as usual. And worse. We removed the 10 commandments from the courthouse in Alabama, but more, from our hearts. While a judge who upholds God's law was condemned and fired, a San Francisco court and mayor are applauded for BREAKING state law on gay marriage! This is INSANE, truly a fulfillment of the Prophet's words that men will call good evil, and evil good. We are far more spiritually corrupt than we were BEFORE 9/11, like the Proverbs said, a dog returning to its own vomit. As much as I despise Al Qaeda and reject Islam, one has to wonder: Seeing who we are, what our media does, the pornography and flesh-peddling we support, may there in fact not be a reason that those who gaze at us from Islamic nations see us as "The Great Satan"? Our hypocrisy was so clear to me in the days following 9/11 when I saw a sign over a strip bar saying, "God bless America." He will not bless such national hypocrisy, and the edge of judgment is drawing near.

I am neither democrat nor republican. But from a long-range perspective, this is what I see: Most political and media pundits are saying the elections are about the economy and the war. "Peace and Prosperity." As said two decades ago, "It's the economy, stupid!"

Is it?

It is absolutely NOT. If you vote your pocketbook, God help you. How much are you for sale for? This kind of national view exposes the real heart of selfishness in us. It's all about US. OUR desires, OUR lust for more, OUR "rights". (Rights used to mean our freedom to do the RIGHT thing – not our arrogance thinking no one can deny us anything WE want.) Such short-sighted selfishness will lead to disaster in a life, in a nation.

Elections are not the issue. It is about the spirit of lawlessness which is overtaking our land. Laws are now being made to challenge, overthrow and denigrate God's Law. Do I need to draw you a clearer picture? GAY MARRIAGE? Banning the 10 commandments? Slaughtering babies? September 11th may have been a door of grace to see if we would truly turn to God. God must be fair. He has determined of Himself to go the distance with us before He allows us to implode, and I believe He has. It is NOT about the economy. It is about SPIRITUAL BANKRUPTCY.

It will not be long in coming that will begin to set in motion a large-scale attack on churches, evangelism and truth-tellers who WILL NOT BE SILENT OR SILENCED. Prepare for that.

It has been a revelation to hear two of the former political candidates, with an almost evangelistic presentation, denounce fundamentalist Christians as the enemy of this country. It is just a small taste of what is to come.

Recently France moved to pass a law forbidding Muslim women to wear headscarves in schools. If you are rejoicing, don't. They also have forbidden the wearing of Kippas (yarmulkes) or stars of David, or crosses in public places. It is just the beginning. The day will come – perhaps precipitated by another large-scale terrorist attack by Islamic terrorists on our country – that it will be decided that ANY religious display or evangelism in public is

ILLEGAL, and that ANY religious expression in public is dangerous and needs to be banned. Obviously, they will reason, we can't just discriminate against Muslims, right? So EVERYONE will have to conform. The problem is, in fact CHRISTIANS are the only ones who are COMMANDED TO BE PUBLIC AND EVANGELIZE! And where will that leave us? Either doing what most believers do now, unfortunately – not evangelizing AT ALL – or BREAKING A LAWLESS LAW. I for one have no intention of "keeping my religion to myself." Neither should you, though I can promise you that the price of evangelism and truth-telling is about to go up.

Even now, those who are not afraid to speak to truth in or out of church are being categorized: "Divisive. Non-inclusive." And the newest buzzword, "The Haters." That's right. Christians are being called "the haters" by more and more people. And why? Because they LOVE THE TRUTH and are not afraid to challenge the lies. You who cherish God's Word and God's law will be called the haters by the lawless ones. Get used to it and more. And we ARE haters. We hate SIN. We hate SICKNESS. We hate poverty and drug addiction and sexual perversions of all kinds and pride and sensuality and pornography and child abuse and death. And it is because we LOVE the lost humanity Jesus died to save. So we hate everything that is murdering THEM. They cannot, and will not see that. "And this is the condemnation, that light has come into the world, and men loved darkness rather than light, because their deeds were evil." Do not expect people to thank you for being truth-tellers: expect them to hate you for that, except for those for whom the light of truth is a deliverance from darkness and evil. Most will only see that you are a bigot, sexist, homophobic, fundamentalist, a "hater". I promise you, the spirit of lawlessness that has mass-brainwashed this world despises you already.

So do we hide? Circle the wagons? Enjoy church and hope we don't get caught? Worse, hope that we are not FORCED to publicly PROCLAIM JESUS? God forbid it! It is now that God is desiring to raise up a generation of truth-tellers who will throw caution and danger to the wind to "proclaim the truth with all boldness." We must pronounce a death sentence on "apologize evangelism." NEVER ONCE did Jesus or the apostles preface their word with, "I'm not trying to offend you." Neither should we. Jesus did not stand and say, "Every head bowed, every eye closed, no one looking around…we don't want to embarrass anyone." NO! He said, "Follow me and do it publicly. It will cost you your lives. Do not follow unless you are willing to give all." The Gospel is by nature an OFFENSE to all those who do not love the truth.

It is at this critical juncture in history that we will either have the spirit of Stephen, who spoke the truth as it pierced the heart of the people, causing them to rage and even gnash their teeth and costing Stephen his life, or we will cower behind the unconverted Peter's words, "I DO NOT KNOW THE MAN!" This is what lies ahead for us.

I pray that this generation, especially youth, will be given a holy boldness to speak the truth of Jesus. Speak it in the classrooms, speak it in the universities, speak it on your jobs, among your friends, speak it and DO NOT HOLD BACK. Dare to go against the current of lies and speak truth, no matter how unpopular it is, no matter how ridiculed it is, no matter what threats may come. Throw the gauntlet of truth down NOW while it is still day, "For the night is coming when no man can work." Then when the night comes, you will still be speaking truth, and not cowering in a corner afraid someone will know that you are a believer. Before it is over, we will each be forced to either deny the Lord that bought us or to proclaim His power and truth. May God grant you the spine and the strength to make that decision in the LIGHT so that you will not deny the truth in the darkness to come.

4 LIKE ALL THE OTHERS (OR, WHY WE HAVE NO POWER)

"…That we may be like all the nations." (1 Samuel 8:20)

Nobody likes to not fit in. Billions of dollars are spent on advertising each year, in fact, to tell us how to fit in. You need these clothes, that video game, this music CD, these shoes, that car. Culture does not create the marketplace. The market creates the culture. We are told on a continual basis what we need to be cool, the "it" thing, successful, healthy. And the more we do things to be "different," the more we look just like the rest of the herd.

One thing I love about God is that He doesn't want us to be anything but what we are – who we are – in our hearts. I wish we knew this.

Christian music is getting weaker and weaker because we "want to be like all the nations." Unless a miracle happens, I may have bought my last Christian CD. I can't stand the shallowness of it anymore. It all sounds just like the world's music, only with insipid, shallow Christian feel-good lyrics. In our desire to create music the world can "relate" to, we've left out the Creator who can make music the world is ASTOUNDED by.

When is the last time you played a Christian CD for an unbeliever and they were astounded, or said, "Wow! That got my HEART!"

There was a time, you know. There was a man named Keith Green, who was about to become a music superstar. He found Jesus and poured his life into writing and singing about Him. He sounded and wrote like NO ONE ELSE, not in the world, not in the church. His songs burned with the convicting power of GOD. People left his concerts either angry, or changed forever.

There was a band called "The 2nd Chapter of Acts." It was three skinny kids, who, when they sang, leveled audiences. Everyone knew their lyrics and harmonies were not human. They were angelic. From the moment they sang, the power of God descended and crowds were caught up in devastating worship. They weren't slick, they didn't dress cool. They were just VESSELS OF THE HOLY.

I weep when I listen to what is produced today. It is STERILE. It is lifeless. Well-intentioned, but lifeless. In striving to sound like the world, we have succeeded fabulously. But there is no power to redeem.

Music and worship are so important to God that He sent the worshipers first onto the battlefield. How can we expect to see lives changed if we don't create music with that kind of gravity? How can a Christian musician hope to be anything but a passing fad, unless they come close enough to the Holy of Holies to at least be brushed with the wings and winds of the Holy angels?

No, we can only have it two ways; either to "be like other nations" or cry out for His anointing on our music, career or not.

You won't make many friends that way. One of the other "prophets of music" was Steve Camp, whose first albums were wildly successful, fun things. Then he got serious. He wrote songs about commitment, sacrifice, suffering, and the cross. I went to a concert here, watched the 500 or so people party while he sang his fun stuff – then watched ¾ of them get up and walk out when he sang and challenged them to surrender everything. By not "being like the other nations," he lost his shallow audience – but gained a Friend.

There's no space to write extensively about Christian books, but it's the same concept. Shallow, fun, sensational and romantic books sell. Books with depth either tank or never see the light of day. Secular trends become our own, and our best sellers are "just like the other nations," but nicer, with a nice "Jesus touch."

The church has grown trendy, hip, multimedia, seeker friendly, more comfortable. It's hard to tell many church services from an Amway convention these days. We wanted to reach (impress) the world using their methods and their tools, but there is little conviction, there is no challenge, there is no sacrifice. Just a nice place to go once or twice a week, a place we leave unchanged.

We recently had a youth Bible study where God walked in totally unexpectedly and began to put His finger on things we were holding on to from the world. It wasn't fun, it hurt, it was scary. But it was real. I left thinking, "This is what's missing." Most youth ministries are bent on attracting the world through fun, excitement, and a cool trendy youth pastor, so we can "relate" to the world and they to us. "Just like the other nations." But what is needed is the power of God present and working in youth groups through real worship and the pure Word. If we do not set a higher standard, it's just fun and games, youth babysitting. Lives will not be changed. Just modified. Nicer kids, but not transformed kids.

God has called us to be a "peculiar people." Not weird. Although, if we take Him seriously, we'll be unlike anyone or anything the world has seen. We cannot become life-changing people until we LET GO of the longing for success, popularity, likeability, numbers or acceptance. We must give up all the desire to be "like the other nations."

God is calling a generation who want to be NOTHING like the other nations, who despise their trinkets, deny their lures, and have no desire to imitate their trends. He's calling those who will enter the Holy Place to receive eternal music and worship, write with the words of the prophets, preach like Paul and walk in supernatural miracles like it was a common walk. Come up higher, saints. Let go of the world and all its loves. Give Him all, and expect His all – and watch God change the world!

5 ENEMIES OF THE CROSS

I'm an old veteran of the church trend wars that have ebbed and flowed since I began in ministry in 1973. Can a Christian have a demon? Do you have to speak in tongues? Is the rapture going to happen before the tribulation?

Agree to disagree, I concluded. We'll never solve all the conflicts. Focus on the work of the Gospel.

But what happens when one of these issues becomes so harmful that it becomes a malignant beast that threatens to undermine the work of the Gospel? Then I feel it has to be addressed, and I will make few friends in the effort.

The issue is concerning the extreme prosperity gospel.

Even though I objected to the way that the prosperity preachers ignored certain scriptures and took others out of context, I realized that arguing was an exercise in futility. Plus, some of my dearest and most godly friends believe wholeheartedly in that gospel. I could agree to disagree.

All that changed this year. It began when I learned of someone trying to raise support for a very worthy but struggling outreach who was told by some in the prosperity church, "We only give to the 'already blessed.'" Was this the newest mutation of an already shaky doctrine?

What moved me to write this was a conversation I had with a young man who had spent seven years in leadership training directly under the pastors of one of the largest prosperity churches in the state. What he saw and experienced led him to finally walk away – from the church – from Jesus.

He was not bitter, nor did he speak to "get back" at them. He simply conveyed, because I asked, his experience to me. This is a sampling:

- The pastors lived in a luxurious house in one of the most well-to-do areas of their low-income city.

- Most of their congregation is poor to lower middle-income people fed weekly on a diet of “you too can be rich”.

- The church just installed a $125,000 coffee bar in the church.

- The Pastor’s fee to travel to teach other pastors how to raise tithing and their income is $20,000 a day plus first-class everything.

- The Pastors complained about and laughed at their staff and the struggling poor people who they often used, for little or no wages, as maids, bodyguards, gardeners, etc.

His most startling statement when I asked him how they could follow God and justify all this was, “God? I don’t think these people believe in God at all. It’s not about God to them. It’s a business. That’s it.”

It angered me that a promising young leader was now an assistant to a professor that taught that the Bible was nothing but a myth. I could not dismiss all of this as just the bitter rantings of a disgruntled church goer, which is the usual self-defense we use to justify our wrongs as leaders. His was actually just the latest in a fifteen-year stretch of horror stories coming from that church.

The last straw for me was learning that one of the most popular Christian preachers and mega-selling author had come to that church – for a fee of $50,000 a night plus first class everything.

When did the ministry become a place of privilege, prosperity, power and prestige? Why aren’t we outraged, when, as I write this, thousands of missionaries around the globe are spilling their life blood to reach the lost without thought to pay, while the spiritual elite in the U.S. are living lives of obscene, pampered wealth? And how did we become so used to it that we EXPECT to pay big bucks for ministry?

What happened to “freely you have received, freely give”?

I recently traveled to Ohio to speak at a youth rally. The coordinator said, “What do you need?” “Travel & hotel, maybe a love offering,” I replied. “What else?” he asked. What does he mean, what else? “I don’t know, some bottled water onstage?” “That’s it?” he laughed. That’s it. He explained that most of the preachers and speakers they got had a high fee, demanded limos, first class hotels, fruit baskets, you name it. Just like Hollywood stars or rock bands. I felt sick.

When you watch Christian TV, listen to Christian radio or read Christian magazines, you come to realize that we've developed a ministry caste system. The haves and the have-nots. The happening and the has-been. The apostles, bishops and self-proclaimed prophets who take out full page ads...and the struggling little preacher who can only afford a tiny little ad so he can send out free Gospel tracts. Just like India. The rich...and the Untouchables.

And what, largely, do the Ministries of the Rich and Famous offer? Large Christian feeding troughs – expensive spiritual buffets of spiritual junk food designed to make you prosper, feel good, get blessed and get more. And you get, get, get, only when you give, give, give – to THEM. The Gospel is little more than a ticket to the Good Life. And it flies in the face of not only the complete and consistent truth of the scriptures, but of the millions of martyrs and saints who gave ALL so others could just find Jesus. No price was too much for them to pay, no sacrifice too great.

We should be mortified. I am sure that the Great Cloud of Witnesses is.

I am not against wealth, and poverty is not a virtue. I certainly am not against large ministries, or ministers being worthy of their hire. And like Paul, I've been abased, and abounded. I have met ridiculously generous rich believers who can never stop giving, and I have met poor people who are going to hell for the love of money. It's not about what you have, but what is at the center of your life, your heart, your affections.

But I cannot believe that much of modern evangelical Christianity has become little more than big business in the guise of a spiritual "move of God" whose Kingly leaders shell out plastic trinkets and call it Gold – or God – or the Gospel. And all we get is – fat. And lazy.

Most of this empire has been built on two verses:

"Beloved, I pray that you would prosper in all things and be in health, even as your soul prospers." (3 John 2)

This, we are told, is proof that God wants you to be rich. But in fact, "May you prosper in all things and be in health" was simply a common greeting of the time, much like us saying, "Have a nice day" or "May God bless and keep you" at the end of a letter. This is hardly a sound prooftext to prove

God wants us to be rich.

"Whatever he does shall prosper." (Psalm 1:3b) This verse, the first part of a Psalm contrasting the godly with the wicked, is used as proof God wants you to prosper. But the word "prosper" in Hebrew simply means, "push forward." Progress. Growth. In our total lives. Again, one verse, taken out of context. And as with the verse above, they are using "prosper" to only mean "money," which these writers clearly never intended.

Other verses, however, provide the full truth: "Freely you have received; freely give." (Matthew 10:8) Isn't it self-evident that charging exorbitant fees to preach God's free Word is not just a sin, but a scandal, a shame?

"Set your affections on things above, and not on things of the earth." (Colossians 3:2) When we seek for wealth, it becomes an idol and Jesus is dethroned.

"He who is the greatest among you, let him be as the younger, and he who governs as he who serves." (Luke 22:26) Jesus said not to seek the best seat, the head of the table. He warned his leaders NOT to Lord it over the flock, but to be SERVANTS. Paul did not ride around in a stretch chariot charging big fees. Most often he paid his own way, even while teaching that a laborer was worth his hire. In fact he paid his own way to avoid appearance that he was using the Gospel for money. Shouldn't we?

But let's look at that. Do you really believe ministers and Christian speakers are worth fees that often make their worldly corporate counterparts blush? Who do we think we are? Even the world laughs at us. We are portraying the farthest thing from servanthood, humility and guilelessness that we possibly could. Paul said the Apostles were the least, the "offscouring of all things." Not pampered, privileged, powerful and rich.

I believe Paul spoke to our crisis when he said there were those "who suppose that godliness is a means of gain. From such withdraw yourself. Now godliness with contentment is great gain. For we brought nothing into this world, and it is certain we can carry nothing out. And having food and clothing, with these we shall be content." Do you really think Paul would be anything less than appalled at what is being taught? What else can this be, but speaking to those who preach "the Gospel is about gain" and build empires from offerings ?

While hundreds of millions of dollars are filling the coffers of those who live lavish lives while giving lip-service to "reaching the lost", the REAL world languishes in darkness while a vast army of missionaries – here and abroad – stand ready to give all but struggle because the resources are being misdirected to build self-serving empires far from the battle, or from suffering, or from even the slightest hint of self-sacrifice for the highest call. Paul called these "enemies of the cross" in Philippians 3:18-19. Read it for yourself and tell me it does not apply.

There will always be plenty of people who will follow these teachings and teachers blindly, because they appeal to people's basest flesh instincts and covetousness. But the time has come for the church to pull out its support from them.

Do not buy their books. Do not purchase their overpriced seminar tapes. Do not attend their conferences, and do not fall prey to their seductive words when they tell you, "God is telling me that if you sow $1000 into this ministry, He will answer your prayers." No, He will not! He will answer because He loves you – because of His mercy. You cannot buy His gift (doesn't this form of manipulation remind you of the "indulgences" once sold by the church?) and hear me – GOD WILL NOT BE MANIPULATED.

When you are broken, sick, hurting and jobless, and the TV preacher reaches into your hurt with tears and says, "I sense someone is hurting...if you reach for your checkbook and give your best gift..." just dry your tears, shut that huckster off and write a check for someone or some cause that REALLY needs it – someone worse off than you. Do it, not because you think it will trigger some divine chain reaction financially, or that God will feel He owes you now. Do it because it is a command to give, especially to the needy and poor. Do it to break the chain of despair and depression you may feel. Do it and LAUGH because God WILL take care of all you need! He can create from nothing. Do it to scorn the very idea that God needs our money at all. Do it to starve the hucksters that would tap your vulnerability and suck you dry to make themselves rich.

If this article makes you angry, I cannot apologize. Truth must hurt before it heals. These words, if they anger and hurt us into action, whether we've been deceived by lies, taken by thieves or just ashamed of the way the Gospel is being peddled and merchandised like Madison Avenue, may move us to clean house, kick out the money changers and become the servant-church that we are called to be.

6 HIDDEN MANNA

I bought a study Bible last year. It was full of notes, maps, and commentary. It was a mistake for me to get it. Everything was a distraction, and worse, denominationally bent. I won't be using that one this year!

This year, I bought a giant print, column-in-the-middle, no comment Bible. That's more like it! Clean, silent, waiting…just me, and God's Word.

At this stage in my life, I'm not much interested anymore in commentary – especially since the vast majority of it is achingly shallow. There is a depth to scriptures that most Christian writers haven't even come close to uncovering. Statistics and doctrinal things are fine and useful, but you can have all of that and never really touch the living, breathing heart of God in the Scriptures. And I want THAT above all and anything else.

"To him who overcomes I will give some of the hidden manna to eat." (Revelation 2:17)

The Word of God contains the Hidden Manna. It is provision, food, sustenance and life. But the scriptures are hidden and veiled to both unbelievers and to many believers. It will not yield its secrets and depths to the casual passer-by. It will only open up to the hungry of heart.

There were several items put within the Ark of the Covenant. The Ten Commandments, the rod of Aaron, and some of the manna from the wilderness. The Ark was in the Holy of Holies. In the same way, those who dwell in the outer courts or even the inner court of the house of God will not find this treasure. Only when one comes to the Holy Place and then the Holy of Holies of God's presence do they find the true bread of God.

In my earlier, desperate days as a Christian, I was so wounded and bound that I bought hundreds of Christian books seeking answers. It was a huge waste of time and money. In fact, of those hundreds, only a handful remains: AW Tozer; Amy Carmichael; Rick Howard; Henry Drummond. Their common bond? They had discovered the Hidden Manna and shared it. Almost without exception, all the rest of what I read was just fluff.

It's not that I am a deep thinker. I am just hungry. And it is discouraging to see the vast library of Christian junk food being offered as "deeper truth." The hottest seller in the last decade contains information so basic that it hurts, but it is being touted as REVOLUTIONARY! Something's wrong here. I am afraid we are at a point where Paul would say, "For though by this time you ought to be teachers, you need someone to teach you again the first principles of the sayings of God; and you have come to need milk and not solid food. For everyone who partakes only of milk is unskilled in the word of righteousness, for he is a babe. But solid food belongs to those who are of full age…" (Hebrews 5: 12-14a) How is it that we have believers five, ten, fifteen years old in the Lord who are just now "getting" the basic principles they should have had established in year one?

In any event, I am determined to go after that Hidden Manna. Not for "answers". I have not found the Bible to be some formula, a spiritual 8-ball. That is not its purpose.

Again, the problem with a lot of books is that they present themselves as a guide to answers to life's problem with a scriptural attachment or framework. In short, they say, "This is how to apply verses to make your life work better." You CAN do that; the Bible certainly has the best and only true guidance to everyday life.

But I believe we should rather be saying, "This is how to apply your LIFE to the SCRIPTURE." The Bible is not a cure-all, Band-Aid how-to manual. It is the straight edge truth that we must line up our life to. Our life is not the center of the universe, and the scripture an all-purpose fix-it tool. The SCRIPTURE is the centerpoint, and our lives are to increasingly come nearer to the Jesus-like ideal we see there. This is how we are conformed to the image of His Son.

Attaching Jesus and the Word of God as a sidekick to our life will not get us there. Only when HE and His Word are the Main Event of all we are and do can we ever hope for more than a shallow faith and an unfruitful spiritual life.

I am convinced that God allows times of stress, pressure, pain and difficulty in order to turn our hearts toward His Word. Not so much to find answers, but to find Him.

There has never been a crisis I have faced but that His Word has not brought comfort, strength and encouragement. But not often "answers." Many times, I've cried out to God, searching for an answer, and He has been as likely to say, "Look at the sunset I made, child. Isn't it beautiful?" Completely circumventing my request, and instead raising my sites to His glory and love where answers no longer matter. The Word of God has become the Door to the intimate place of His Heart for me. If all we ever got were answers, would we even seek a relationship with God? No, that's Santa, not a Savior.

God DOES answer us. And He does answer prayers. But He LONGS for us to seek Him, not for answers, but for intimate friendship. And when we do, His Word becomes a feast of joy and fulfillment.

There are three layers to the Scriptures. One is the written word. The unbeliever reads and makes little or no sense of it. It is hidden, until a heart seeks or is born again. Nevertheless, every word is true and will remain forever. But the Word to the unbeliever is just the outer court.

The second layer opens to the believer, filling them, refreshing, strengthening them and challenging them. It becomes real, practical, absolute.

But beyond that layer is a miracle of symphony and perfection. As God's Word is nurtured in your heart and takes root, it begins to change you. And if you come to the well daily, seeking, hungry, insistent, the Scriptures become ALIVE. It will speak less to your "situations" and all to your HEART. It will expose the things of the heart, impurities, evil motives, hidden things. And then it cleanses. As it cleanses, your vision clears and your heart is elevated into higher things and higher purposes, eternal things. God is waiting for you there.

The miracle is that God could condense so much of Himself into one book. The wonder is that its depth will take you so deep into God that you are lost in Him. Every verse connects with all the others you have hidden in your heart before. God can now intimately whisper to you the thoughts and desires of His own heart.

Those who come casually to this well for a hasty sip will never know the Hidden Manna. And it will not yield that Manna easily.

Come to His Word determined to be given this Bread. Seek and keep seeking. Knock and keep knocking! STAY until that Door is open to you where His banquet of truth and life awaits you.

Father, I am hungry. I'm tired of spiritual food that is empty and unsatisfying. I come asking to receive the Hidden Manna. I don't just want answers. I need YOU. Whatever it takes, Father, take me from the shallow waters of facts and quick fix verses and pull me relentlessly into the depths of Truth. Catch me up in the awesome magnificence of Your Word, and let it burn, and cleanse, and transform me. Make me unsatisfied with anything less. Make me an overcomer worthy of receiving Your Hidden Manna. In Jesus' Name, Amen.

7 PURSUE…OVERTAKE…RECOVER

I am so stirred by an Old Testament story I read this morning. When you read a passage, and your heart beats fast, and tears come to your eyes, you know God is present and speaking to your life.

David was running from King Saul. Saul's jealousy and hatred had driven David into exile, where he lived and roamed among Saul's enemies. David had a ragknot army and little in this world. But he clung to God with all he had.

While David and his army were away, the Amalekites came and took everything away, the little he had left. In many ways, I think this was a breaking point for David. For years, he had graciously accepted his life of "downward mobility." He adapted. He forgave Saul. He wept.

Now, he'd had enough. He called for the Ephod, and asked God: "Should I pursue?" "Pursue," God replied, "Overtake them and recover all." That was all David needed. He gathered his men, pursued the Amalekites, overtook them, and recovered all his possessions.

There is a continual assault against all those who long to serve God with a whole heart. Satan prefers Christians to stay right where they are – half-hearted, happy to do little, not radical, just....content to remain where they are.

When someone pursues God and His Kingdom plan, discontent with just getting by spiritually, dissatisfied with regurgitated junk food messages and shallow expectations of God, they get the devil's full attention. He immediately goes into battle mode. He is an expert in the weapons of discouragement, failure, hopelessness, weariness and disappointment.

And frankly, we tend to be very passive about these attacks. The least spiritually mature will say, "This must be God's will." Some will adapt to the constant barrage of attacks on their every effort to serve God, grow and bear fruit and accept it as just "normal expected attacks." But if they continue long enough, these attacks can produce a numbness that becomes crippling and debilitating. The danger is in adapting to the point where you become accustomed to the slow eradication of your spiritual strength, vision and fight. This is such an effective strategy: The rock the hammer won't break, time and tide wears away. Or as one friend put it, it's not the mountain before you that defeats you but the pebble in your shoe.

When you receive enough blows, big and small, you begin to think that is all there is. God's promises seem to be for others, not for us. We adjust, we adapt; some eventually just give up. They love God. But they are spiritually punch-drunk and just can't fight anymore.

Then Satan comes in a comforting voice and soothes, "It's okay! Just stop fighting. Give up. Just settle here where it's safe." And so, great vision and promise become a faded memory. But the enemy is not through with you yet! He wants more. He wants it ALL.

Listen to this astonishing passage from 1 Kings chapter 20: "Thus says Ben-Hadad: Your silver and your gold are mine. Your loveliest wives and children are mine." Ben-Hadad, the king of Syria, made a direct and dire threat to King Ahab. He said, I'm taking your money, and your family. Sound familiar? The two biggest attacks on families, especially on those in ministry, are on their finances and on their home life, their marriage, their children!

Apparently King Ahab had adapted and gotten used to attacks! His reply? "My Lord, O King, just as you say, I and all I have are yours." He just GAVE UP! No fight, no struggle. Just a weary, "Sure, take them. I'm not going to fight."

But that was just the beginning. Ben-Hadad saw the weakness and came in for the rest. He sent a second message: "...I will send my servants tomorrow, and they're going to go through all your things, and WHATEVER is pleasant, whatever you love, they are going to take it away from you."

You see, Satan will rob you of everything if he can. He will wear you out with little attacks, then keeps turning up the heat as you adjust and grow accustomed to it. He makes you numb, unable to fight. You stand by and watch the slow erosion of your life and vision, completely helpless. Then, BAM! He ruins your finances, alienates your spouse and tries to destroy your kids. At some point, the pain and weariness are too much and we say, "Okay. There's nothing I can do. I give up."

And that is when Satan moves in for the kill. Like Ben-Hadad, he says, "I'm not happy with your 'stuff' and your precious little family being destroyed. I want it ALL. Anything and everything that you love, or gives you joy, or turns your heart to God, I will destroy. I'll destroy even your vision and the very call of God on your life. There will be nothing left when I'm done with you!"

I've met so many Christians that came to this moment and simply folded. They lost everything and became hollow shells without even a glimmer of light left. This is the deciding moment when we must either roll over and let Satan take it all, or WAKE UP and say, "No! I've had enough! No more!" And we begin to fight back.

Israel's king finally said, "THIS I cannot do." He became enraged and sent this message: "The gods do so to me, and more also, if enough dust is left of Samaria for a handful for each of the people that follow me." In other words, he said, "Not only am I not going to let you take anything from me, but by the end of this, YOU won't have anything left. I'm coming for you!"

Just like David when his family and possessions were taken, Ahab had been pushed too far – the enemy overplayed his hand – and up from his gut came a roar of rage, and he got hold of God and brought great retribution on the enemy.

Deep down, there is something in us that is screaming against all the bondage, robbery and paralyzation the enemy has put on us. Like Gulliver, we are God's giants tied down, not with a huge chain but with thousands of little ropes of fears and bondage and attacks we have let accumulate through neglect or regret. Rise up, child of God! It is time to break those chains and make the enemy pay. Pursue. Overtake. Recover all!

In a moment long ago of absolute spiritual clarity, in a time of failure and hopelessness when Satan had robbed me of all I held dear, including my vision and heart for ministry, I looked into the eyes of a fallen believer as he said, "Just give up. Stop fighting. God doesn't want you to struggle anymore." And I saw the eyes and soul of Satan himself and I understood the whole plan that had defeated my life. He'd taken so much of what I loved, and now he wanted me to lie down and let him take the rest! And inside, I saw a vision of myself, a bloody mess on a boxing ring floor, and a scream so guttural and primal came from my spirit and said, "NO! NEVER! I will die first before I surrender ONE MORE INCH OF TERRITORY TO YOU, SATAN!" And I rose up from that boxing floor and pummeled the enemy to a bloody pulp. From that moment on, I pursued and overtook the enemy and began to recover all he had stolen from me. And vigilance is the constant cost of that victory.

There is a life worse that constant conflict. It is a life of numb complacency, of a life of light grown accustomed to the darkness of defeat, the comfort of an end of the struggling.

I saw a movie in which a warrior asked another, "What do you fear?" The reply burned into my spirit and brought me to tears: "A cage. To stay behind bars until use and old age accept them, and all chance of valor has gone beyond recall or desire."

Nothing should frighten us more than the sad prospect of such a meaningless end to God's glorious plan for our lives. We were born for battle, for valor, and for victory. We are called to be free, and freedom-fighters, and more than conquerors. Take up your sword, my friend! Pursue. Overtake. Recover all!

8 SHOCK AND AWE

As we engaged Iraq in the first war of the new Millennium, the military spoke frequently and emphatically about the coming "Shock and Awe" phase of the military operation. Most everyone scratched their heads at this peculiar phrase.

In the Hebrew traditions, there is a word that is used to define the cloud of God's glory: It is roughly translated as "Shekinah" but the Hebrew mystics wrote it as "SHKNH". Shock and awe. It is highly probable that the strategists in the Psychological Warfare division of the army, who have a flair for the dramatic as well as the mystic and sometimes occultic, knew full well that the entire middle east would understand perfectly what "Shock and Awe" meant. When they added the new bomb, the "Mother of All Bombs" – "Moab" – I saw the picture. Moab was the sworn enemy of Israel, and was completely destroyed.

As I was thinking about this clever use of words, it struck me that "shock and awe" does indeed describe the true power of God.

I remember as a young believer when the Holy Spirit was doing incredible things among large groups of people, specifically youth, I heard several teachers and pastors refer to the "shekinah" glory of God. It was the Cloud of God's Presence that descended and rendered everyone awestruck, powerless and stunned.

As with many of my dearly loved and tightly held spiritual ideas, it was only last month when I discovered that the word Shekinah was NOT in the Bible! It is from Jewish mystical writings. But the REALITY of Shekinah is VERY scriptural:

"And it came to pass, when the priests came out of the Holy (place) that the cloud filled the house of the Lord, so that the priests could not stand to minister because of the cloud; for the Glory of the Lord filled the house of the Lord." (1 Kings 8:10)

Can you imagine what it must have been like, for God's Presence to be so overwhelming that they couldn't even stand up?

There is a reason God had to hide His full Presence (face) from Moses, and even though Moses only saw part of Him, he had to cover his face it was shining so bright with God's Glory! (Exodus 34:29-31)

Shock and awe, indeed.

I have been blessed on several occasions to experience that kind of Divine Unveiling Presence. I'd like to tell you about just three.

When I was at Bible School, we had a special chapel speaker who taught on prophetic worship and song. As she led us through several worship songs, the entire atmosphere of the auditorium began to change. Like the surging and receding of waves on the shore, the worship would rise, fall, rise higher, until it built into a crescendo so overwhelming that it sounded like a million voices at once. Then, nothing – just a terrible, Holy silence – followed by a heavy Cloud of Presence that rendered the 600 plus students – myself included – speechless, shaking, and prostrate on the floor. I feared to move, hiding my head covered with hands under the seat in front of me.

Before it was over, several hours had passed!

Shock and Awe.

The second time, I was attending chapel at the tiny live-in center of Youth Defenders, a ministry for brain damaged kids. It was my first ministry position. I was nineteen.

I had almost not gone that night. But while sitting in the service, my mind was taken from the Pastor's words by specific scriptures from the book of Acts that came roaring into my mind. I opened my Bible and found each one – each one dealing with anointing, calling, being called out and sent forth and ordained for the work of the ministry. And each time I found the specific verse God was speaking to me, the pastor read the exact same verse! One scripture after another, I would find and the Pastor would read and expound on – except I was too shaken to hear – I began to literally shake all over from the Presence I felt descending on me. The Presence descended on the entire chapel, and the Pastor began to weep under the power of the Presence and suddenly exclaimed, "I can't continue! Greg, come forward; we are to lay hands on you and commission you for the work of the ministry!" I RAN – but I never made it to the raised platform where the Pastor was. I ended up at the bottom stair, my face buried in the carpet, so terrified by this awesome Presence that I dared not look up! I wept and trembled as they lay hands on me and sent me forth as the scriptures command.

That was shock and awe. God unexpectedly showed up and changed my destiny and direction forever.

The third time, I was in the privacy of my bedroom. It was a time when I had suffered deep personal losses and was burned out and crippled with an overwhelming sense of personal failure in my life and my ministry. I was near to quitting altogether.

I had not felt God's love in so long, I had become a hollowed out shell, empty and lost. "Father," I cried quietly, "I need You. I need to FEEL Your love, or I'm not going to make it."

In a few moments, I felt Him approach, and I felt Him hovering over me. I began to weep and to worship Him. His Spirit touched me, touched my body, my burnt emotions, my fractured mind. The presence of pure love enveloped me until my whole body felt, what? Overpowered is such a weak word to describe it. His love grew stronger as I worshipped, and soon I was caught up in a Presence so strong I could not move a muscle. Stronger it became, stronger, stronger! I felt at that moment that if He drew any nearer, I would simply vacate my body and be translated into heaven in one instant! "No more, Jesus, please!" I cried out. "I can't take anymore! Please, it's too much!" And He lovingly withdrew Himself, leaving me both revived and shaken to my foundation.

Now, that was shock and awe!

You know, I know we think we know what we're asking for when we ask for the power of God, for His Glory to fall in our midst. But we really don't.

I always am very wary of people that say they see angels, hear God's voice and see visions like it was nothing at all, just flippantly talking like they're telling you what they ate for lunch. I wonder if they are hearing God at all. Do you know why?

Because when God showed up in the Scriptures, there was rarely any lighthearted, flippant reaction. There was usually terror! Like Daniel, when the Angel of the Lord appeared to him: "...When he came I was afraid and fell on my face...and I, Daniel, fainted and was sick for days..." (Daniel 8:17,27) "...the men who were with me did not see the vision; but a great terror fell upon them, so that they fled to hide themselves...and no strength remained in me; for my vigor was turned to frailty in me, and I retained no strength...while he was speaking I stood trembling...I turned my face to the ground and became speechless... (Daniel 10:7,8,11,15)

Now God did not leave him in that condition; the Angel spoke to him, comforted and strengthened him. But this was no casual encounter; it COST Daniel something physically, and it terrified everyone around him! "But that's Old Testament!", you say. Yes, I know. And I know we can come boldly to the throne of Grace. But when Paul met Jesus, he had an almost identical experience, being knocked off his horse by the power of God! I am sure he never flippantly referred to how God "touched" him!

Do you understand what I am saying? Even Peter, when he saw Jesus transfigured with Moses and Elijah, was heavy with sleep under the Presence, and when he awoke and realized what was going on, he was so dumbstruck that he mumbled something about setting up a tent for them to visit! It even says, "not knowing what he said."

I could go on and on. After Jesus' resurrection, He told the disciples to wait in Jerusalem for the promise of the Holy Spirit outpouring. They waited and prayed, and He was poured out as flames of fire descended on each and all heaven broke loose. The rest of the story is in the book of Acts – resurrections, multitudes saved and healed and delivered, or as it was said, they turned the whole world upside down. You better believe everyone, especially the disciples, were experiencing the shock and awe Presence of God!

It makes me sad for us. We are content with so little from God, really. We're satisfied with a nice sermon, a few well-oiled goosebump-producing songs and a nice potluck, then back to business as usual.

We do not long for more. We do not hunger for it.

On the other hand, we should know what we are asking for when we pray for the Spirit to come. For when He does, if you expect gentle waves of fluffy clouds, beware. Our God is a consuming fire.

When He comes, "His winnowing fan will be in His hand, and he will thoroughly purge his threshing floor." (Matthew 3:12) When He comes, He comes to cleanse, to purify, to make a straight path.

When He comes, it will NOT be business as usual. All bets are off; all potlucks canceled until further notice. We'll find all our planned order of service completely ruined, as Jesus comes with HIS agenda – convicting, healing, transforming. We will cry like the prophet Isaiah: "I am undone!"

I long for and tremble at the prospect of that visitation. I long for it because I am bound by my own mundane struggles, my visionlessness, my sad satisfaction with tiny spiritual snacks and my struggle toward lukewarmness. I long for God's Presence to break apart these shackles of spiritual impotence and carelessness and casualness and in a Paul-blinding moment reorder, redirect and re-anoint my life in such a way that I will never be the same again. I want to be RUINED by God.

We sing the song, "Come, Lord Jesus, come." I am sure that we mean it, at least we mean that we long for Him to come and take us Home.

But my heart has been singing it in a new way: "Come now. Come HERE. Come down in the shock and awe Glory of all that You are, and consume all of me in You, and fill me with everything You are. No matter what it takes, Jesus, come!

And if this becomes our corporate prayer, the world may yet see the kind of shock and awe of God's Power that will once again turn the world upside down!

9 THE DRIVEN LIFE

The church went through a major obsession with the Rick Warren book, "The Purpose Driven Life." The title got me thinking about the word "driven." I want to speak to you about the "driven life."

I don't like texting. It's not enough to be online, have e-mail, and have a cell phone with a hundred sounds and ten inboxes. Now we're swamped with text, Facebook, tweets. It's ridiculous to be at a table with six people and they're all texting and not talking. Sometimes I wanted to scream, "Just pick up the phone and CALL for cryin' out loud!!!" Even though texting may have a few practical applications, I can't help but see it as just another addition to the push to make us human cyborgs, add to our manic lifestyle and keep us from developing REAL relationships. This is the "brave new world" where kids only communicate by quoting movie lines to each other and only share real thoughts and feelings behind the protection of texts and "instant messaging."

I don't like this brave new world. I mean, it's ridiculous. Picture it: here I am in my office: I'm online, doing research with three internet sites opened. I'm trying to answer the 150 or so months-old e-mails that I can never seem to get down to ten. My cell phone rings. Then as I'm talking to the caller, someone else calls; I switch over. It's a recorded ad! And then my office phone rings, and it's a recorded sales call. At that moment, my server dumps 15 more e mails into the folder I've just answered three e mails from – when my cell phone gets an e mail message from someone in Juarez chattering away in a language I still don't get.

This is when the vision comes to me of a huge fire in my backyard piled with my computers, scanner, two printers, cell phone, fax, office phone, and a partridge in a pear tree, as I laugh maniacally at the digital inferno, screaming, "Free at last, free at last!!!"

I mean, how did we LIVE without being so "connected"?

As I recall, we did just fine. Maybe better, in fact, than we're doing now. And isn't it amazing that Jesus and the apostles turned the world upside down without instant messaging? Just think.

And while Microsoft softly asks, "Where do YOU want to go today?", God just picked up Philip by the river after completing his assignment and whisked him off to his next one. Hm.

We are a driven people. We do not rest. We do not reflect. We do not STOP. Our culture is high-gear madness, driven to make everything faster. We are losing our soul to the electronic Beast.

It makes me sad, because Christians are just as driven. I don't WANT a "purpose-driven life". I don't want to be "driven" at all!

Did you notice that the Psalmist didn't say, "You drive me in the paths of righteousness for Your Name's sake"? No; He LEADS us. We follow.

I remember a frightening true story written by a man who, while in Israel, wanted to actually see sheep, a shepherd and a pasture so he could mine the true riches of Psalm 23. As he spoke to a shepherd, he saw a man with a stick driving sheep down a hill. "Why is that shepherd doing that?, he asked. "He is not a shepherd," the man replied. "He has been hired to bring the sheep to the slaughterhouse." What a stunning revelation!

I do not take away from the urgency of the hour by saying this. Jesus said, "Work while it is yet day, for the night is coming when no man can work." We ARE to work in His Kingdom. But it is HIS work that we do, not ours, and there is the problem. We used to sing the old hymn, "Without Him, I can do nothing...." But the sad truth is, without Him we can do PLENTY. And we DO.

Jesus LEADS us to work beside Him. Satan DRIVES us just to "Stay busy for God." As I've often said, if Satan can't get you to do one bad thing, he'll get you to do twenty good things that aren't God's things – things He has NOT led you to do!

With our lives already inundated with techno terror, work and family responsibilities, just add religious busy work, and you are being driven by the devil and you're a candidate for religious burnout.

Wait a minute, you say – I thought we were supposed to burn out for God! Poured out, yes – but NOT burned out.

I once had a ministry friend who couldn't tolerate the fact that I took days off. He told me HE was going to "burn out for God." He was too busy to rest. I reminded him that even Jesus left the crowds to rest and pray. Then I told him about my beloved 2nd car, a VW Beetle that I drove into the ground. I drove and drove and drove, ignoring the pretty red dot flashing on my dashboard. My oil light. (I thought it was kind of a special effects stereo add-on). I burned the engine to a crisp because I ignored the warning light and I never added oil. End of car.

Dad taught me: Change the oil every 2,000 miles, and you can keep a car forever. Since I took his advice, ALL my cars have been long-livers. Even Dad's car I inherited when he died, an '86 Toyota Camry, is still purring at 200,000 miles!

I told my friend – burn out if you want to, but I'm oiling this baby to last for a lifetime. God's temple deserves good care.

Which brings me to another subject. The Shabbat. (That's the Sabbath, for my Goy friends.) Do any Christians REALLY observe it? Observing the Shabbat was a command, you know. God created in six days, rested the 7th. He said, "You do the same." God designed our physical, emotional and spiritual lives to require a day to stop, be with Him, rest. It was so serious that Israel spent 70 years in slavery for continuing to ignore the Shabbat.

This is where grace-o-philes say, "We're not under the law! We're under GRACE! We don't HAVE to!" (No, you GET to.) Okaaay....then why did Paul address it at all? He did NOT say don't keep it. He simply said the DAY is not the issue – it is that you do KEEP a day for God. And frankly, I do have some questions about the switcheroo from Saturday to Sunday, but that's another article...But keeping it is for OUR benefit. Jesus said the Shabbat was made for man, not the other way around. In other words, it's for your blessing. Ignore it if you want, but believe me, you do reap the consequences in many ways.

Which brings me to my next issue. Having been a minister for over 28 years, I can tell you – for Pastors, Sunday is NOT the day of rest! It's hard labor!!! For that reason, every pastor needs to designate another day as their personal Shabbat, disconnect the phone, and STOP. We fail to do so at the cost of their health, relationships, and even anointing.
But the Shabbat is not just for ministers – it is for all of us. And so few of us even give it a serious try. We do not take a day to rest, to pray, enjoy the peace and beauty of God, worship, be with family and friends in God's fellowship. And because we do not, we are driven the rest of the week. And the devil is the driver behind the wheel.

So how do we stop the madness of the devil-driven life and enter into true Shabbat-rest as a lifestyle? (Strive, the book of Hebrews says, to enter into His rest.) How do we ensure that we are truly doing God-led work and not devil-driven busywork?

Here are a few things to consider:

(1) Without having one day committed to rest and honoring God, you have not conditioned your heart, body and mind to receive His leading. You can't be LED while being DRIVEN, and God gives us one day to stop so He can take the lead. A Shabbat day, by the way, is not mowing the lawn, running 100 errands or finishing up office work at home. I know because we're so frantic in the way we live that this seems like just an ideal rather than an attainable goal, but shouldn't we at least give it a try?

(2) Examine your heart & motives for "doing things for God."

- Am I doing things for God just to please others and make a good impression?
- Am I doing it to look spiritual?
- Am I doing it so God will love me more?
- Am I doing busy things for God to avoid the horrible silence and wounds and hurts that silence would reveal if I am still enough, long enough to listen?
- Am I doing it to give me a sense of worth before God?

All of these could be a sign that you are being devil-driven.

I have had to deal with all of these issues at one time. And I still have to fight to maintain my time alone with God, daily, and my day of rest once a week. When I do, everything goes better. I am more productive, less stressed and a much nicer person to be around! If I let that time be taken from me, I have to fight to get anything done.

I have had to learn that my worth to God has nothing to do with what I do for Him. It is a BLESSING to work for Him. And it is a shared labor, a labor of gratefulness and love, one born of the heart and not of panic or a sense of worthlessness. Men especially struggle with this – so much of our sense of worth comes from what we do. And God wants you to know that you are worth just as much to God when you are doing nothing as when you are doing something. My spiritual seasons involve months at a time when I am just WAITING. It is hard. But it is heart-preparation. I would rather wait and know that what I do is given by God, then constantly striving to "make something happen." That is why I determined long ago not to promote myself. The scriptures say that promotion comes from ABOVE. And God has never failed to bring those open doors, when I simply wait and trust.

Father, help us to have done with the driven life. Help us to take time to rest – to honor You in the Shabbat – that we may be fruitful by allowing You to have the best of our time. Help us begin to watch less TV, fewer movies. Help us to listen to the silence where You dwell. Give us the courage not to give in to the many demands that You have not authorized us to respond to. And help us to find our worth, not in what we do for You, but in the fact that you simply love us and chose us to be your children. Divest us of anything and everything that creates a chaotic life and burns us out. Let Your peace rule in our hearts and minds, a peace that only comes from letting You LEAD us – a peace that comes from taking Your yoke on us, and learning from You as we rest in Your holy presence. Help us to know that all good things, and all fruit that remains will be born of a life of quiet confidence that You are leading us, and will not fail to fill our lives with all the meaning and purpose we could ever hope to have.

10 THE MORE I KNOW…

One of the favorite pastimes of Bible School was for us to gather and beat the tar out of each other with the Bible. It was great sport, stimulating, elating, and affirming – of our own particular doctrines, of course, which we were NOW emboldened to preach even more, since our heretic brothers failed to see the light.

I think it was a good thing in many ways. We were cutting our teeth on the Truth. Maybe we had zeal without knowledge (or just enough to be dangerous!) but we were hungry to know. We were filled with adolescent passion and righteous fervor. Later, hopefully, we learned that knowledge puffs up, but love builds up. Some did not, and went on to find whole congregations to brutalize and batter with their "truth". (One of my favorite quotes is, "God said FEED my sheep, not BEAT my sheep!") Unfortunately, a handful of our class went so far in the OTHER direction that they became new age believers that believed in everything, therefore nothing.

It has been a long and wonderful journey discovering God, His Word, and truth. I have prayed hard and beseeched God to keep me from error, from diluting the truth, from losing the passion for truth. I have beseeched Him equally to keep me from becoming a spiritual monster/tyrant that would use scriptures as a bludgeoning weapon, an arrogant "defender of the faith" who knows all and feels the Heretic Cry every time someone's views were not my own.

I've come to know that the more I know, the less I seem to know. And the more SOME things are….unmovable. We used to laugh at our Vietnamese brother in High School Bible Study that would proclaim, "If I know enough to say dat what I know is not enough to say dat I know enough, den what I know is enough. And derefore it is enough." Well, now I know he was right.

Humility is the hallmark of those who seek God's truth. It's admitting we never know it all – and when we begin to think we do, we know NOTHING of the vast nature of God's Word and God's truth.

Doesn't it ever fill you with awe and wonder that the Great God of the Universe, creator of a trillion-gazillion quasars, galaxies and stars, can even begin to distill His truth into one book? It must be like trying to explain quantum physics to an infant. What we have in that book is perfect. What we have in it is all we can handle. What we have in that book is a fragment of all that can be understood of Him humanly, and yet the depth of that Book is unsearchable, eternal, and would take a billion lifetimes to even begin to mine its treasure.

And we think we know it all. At least, a lot of it. Don't we?

The sheer wonder of God's Word is that a single petal of truth ascends into a garden of truth bigger than the universe.

That's why it's not just a book, like the Koran, or the Vedas, or the Book of Mormon or any other religious volume. It is GOD BREATHED. If it were not, how do you explain how one can read one single verse hundreds of times, and then suddenly your eyes are opened and you are breathlessly astonished at a truth you never saw before? Or, like a beautiful diamond, every time you read a verse over the years, a new facet of that gem glimmers that you have never seen before?

When that happens, I understand why the Bible speaks of "trembling at His Word." (Isaiah 66:5) How arrogant of me to think I have a handle on the truth of His Word. What I do know is so little, really – and it makes me hunger for more.

I think we waste so much time on little theological differences. You say potato, I say poTAH to. Unfortunately, in times far past, dissenters were executed over such differences. Unfortunately, in recent times, churches have spiritually butchered each other over issues as small as how to be baptized. Unfortunately, current heresy-hunters, Bible Answer Men and defenders of truth continue the bloody crusade.

In the meantime, millions die without Jesus.

I don't want to waste one second in that mess.

I actually LOVE denominations. The way we are, if we were all in one building, we'd KILL each other.

I've studied the issues of many issues for decades. Half the time, I come up saying, "Gee, I don't know for sure."

But based on my limited knowledge, let me share some of them to illustrate.

1. Is Jesus coming back before, in the middle of, or after the Tribulation?

I haven't a clue. The issue didn't even become controversy until about 100 years ago. I can "prove" all three views Biblically. I WANT to believe He will rapture us before. But I am struck by the woman who asked Holocaust survivor Corrie Ten Boom if Jesus was coming back before the Tribulation. She replied, "Honey, only an American would ask that kind of question." The point: millions of believers worldwide are being jailed, tortured, martyred. WHEN the rapture happens is irrelevant to them; they are already in horrible "tribulation." What matters to them is enduring to the end. For myself, I pray for the best – but am prepared for the worst. And if you disagree, you are still my brother.

2. Full immersion or sprinkle baptism?

Well, for years, I thought full immersion was the only one God recognized. And I still prefer it myself. But one day, I thought about it, and I realized the early persecuted believers met in the catacombs because if they met in public they would be executed. How do you think they baptized new believers? I could be wrong, (I've been wrong many times) but I kind of doubt they had a baptismal tank down there. So maybe that's where sprinkling started. Either way, I just can't wage a holy war over how much water you get. And if you disagree, you are still my brother.

3. Can a Christian have a demon?

Why would you want one?

4. Is speaking in tongues the evidence of being Spirit filled?

Actually, I think LOVE is. And one pastor said TROUBLE is! And many don't believe in tongues at all. I know what I believe. And if you disagree...you are still my brother!

5. How many angels can fit on a head of a pin?

All of them probably.

One of the down sides of being an ace debater in High School is I can win. A LOT. I've had to lay down many a theological debate because, God reminded me, He called me to be a servant, not a politician. There are some issues I feel stronger about than others....like whether you can lose your salvation. (No, I'm not telling you where I stand!)

Too much butchering over that issue. I can "prove" either side. Why waste time arguing about something that the church hasn't resolved for 2,000 years? And there are so many lost and hurting, needing Jesus...

There are some things I know beyond question. There is a real heaven, and a real hell. Jesus is EVERYTHING He said He is. He was born of a virgin. He died for my sins, and rose again the third day. He is coming back.

And, the scriptures are the inerrant Word of God. Don't EVEN try to change my mind about that. After decades of reading and studying that precious Book, it is more real, more alive and more powerful to me than it ever was. It is God's love letter to me, and my owner's manual, my medicine chest and my strongest sword.

These, and a few other things, I know to be true, unchangeable and eternal. Yet, the more I know, the less I know about so much else!

And when my Sunday School kids ask, if I don't have the answer, I say, "I don't have a clue." And watch their astonished faces. ((YOU try telling kids what Ezekiel's "wheel within a wheel" is!) Hey, I won't fake it just to make myself look wise and smart. And neither should you. Only God is all-knowing.

I don't have to know even a fraction of it all. Paul's words, "Knowledge puffs up; love builds up" (I Corinthians 8:1) speaks deeply to me. If I am a spiritual, Biblical know-it-all, then my desire to be right eventually overwhelms my desire to love and to build people up. Worse, the quest for knowledge becomes notches in a gun belt instead of a glorious treasure hunt.

No, I know far less in many ways than I thought I did in my younger years. But the HUNGER stays. It's an incredible adventure – to know HIM – to study HIM – to look deeply into the vastness of His Word. I approach with the innocent wonder of a child discovering the world for the first time.

It is enough to know that my Father knows everything I will ever need to know.

11 THE WORD OF THE LORD

"And the Word of the Lord was rare in those days; there was no widespread revelation." I Samuel 3:1

I have no doubt that we are once again in the times above. The one is completely tied to the other: No Word of the Lord, thus no Revelation. We are aimless and we create programs rather than seek what God wants to do.

What is the Word of the Lord? I will tell you my friends, it is more than the small proof text that is used to build an hour's message of motivational, feel-good material that passes for a sermon in most churches. It is more than three scriptures on tithing meant to turn around a financially failing church. It is SO much more.

I believe the Word of the Lord is the Scripture of God plus the anointing of God spoken with the Authority of God in the Power of God.

I believe 100% in teaching the Word of God. I believe in comforting and encouraging and exhorting with our messages. We have all of that. Or we should. What we are lacking is a fiery Word. A Word that is clear, deliberate and pointed. A Word that is not so pretty.

Pretty messages have the effect of a sedative or an antipsychotic. They make you feel warm and fuzzy, like a pink cloud dream. Soon we feel….alright. Really nice. It's NICE to be a Christian. It feels WONDERFUL!

Years ago I took a nasty 20 foot fall on a ladder, smack onto cement. Once I realized angels weren't there to usher me into heaven, I assessed the damage, and it was not good. Lip bleeding, knee bleeding, stomach pain and my arm grotesquely twisted. It was nearly eighteen hours before I had surgery, and pain doesn't even begin to describe what I felt. Finally a half an hour before surgery, they gave me Demerol, and let me tell you, within thirty seconds, I didn't care if they cut my arm off. Because I didn't feel anything. Just a nice pink cloud of numbness. It felt great! It was so NICE to be in the hospital!

But if they hadn't operated, I would have died. That's a fact. And all the Demerol in the world would not have saved me. It would have only let me die numb. And unaware.

I don't think we realize how far away we are from "The Word of the Lord." It's all about making our life better, our job better, our family better. But God did not intend us to be a self-improvement clinic or a "God-improved" person. He intended nothing less than SPIRITUAL REVOLUTION. And you DON'T get that from warm, fuzzy messages.

I am very concerned about "Seeker Friendly" churches. The basic concept, as I understand it, is that we don't want to scare away or offend unbelievers. So we need to provide a nice, comfortable and contemporary atmosphere. We need to tone down or eliminate altogether the Hellfire stuff. (After all, someone once said, you can catch more flies with honey than vinegar – which caused me to ask why we wanted a church full of flies.) We'll have motivational, practical sermons filled with fun anecdotes, inspirational internet stories and maybe some nice video clips from a secular movie everyone's seen, and then a scripture to make it all work. You know, make the scriptures relevant to our REAL lives. And we won't call Jesus Lord – we'll call Him "leader".

Okay, let's pause here and think really hard.

This Message of Jesus is the message Jesus was crucified for. This is the message that eleven apostles were martyred for. This is the message so powerful that it caused men to cry out, "What must we do to be saved?" This is the message that, in the last century, has caused more slaughter and martyrdom of believers than in the previous 1900 years! And we don't want to OFFEND people? Must we be reminded that the cross is an OFFENSE? My friend, a Gospel that does not WOUND to salvation is not the Gospel at all. It's just....a nice inspirational message. That's ALL.

One of the things that tells me that much of our present day gospel is not the Gospel is the absence of weeping in the church. That's right. Good old-fashioned tears. Where are the tears for, at the first, our own desperate need for God? Then, our tears for the hurting? The lost? The unsaved? Our churches are DRY. We do not hurt, we do not ache and we do not cry. When was the last time you heard "The Word of the Lord" preached and it brought you to broken tears? A very long time, I'll wager.

And why? Because we are not only "seeker friendly, we are "believer friendly." People work hard all week, they don't want to come to church to feel BAD and CRY, do they? So we just make them feel BETTER.

Whose priority are we following?

Many churches are experiencing huge membership growth because people like to feel good when they go to church, and we are accommodating them. Church has become a religious sitcom - a few laughs, some good drama and a nice conclusion.

I venture to say, if we cried out as pastors and people for the Word of the Lord and let it be preached, our churches would empty by half or more.

We desperately need a visitation from God. We do not know it because we have been lulled into complacent pink cloud sleep with spiritual painkillers.

When I read or listen to many contemporary messages, I cannot help but remember a modern day event. Most of you won't remember Andrae Crouch, but he was a powerful black Gospel singer in the 1970's. Andrae was raised by his parents, Pentecostals, in a church in L.A. One night, in the midst of a powerful outpouring of God, the fire department showed up to meet the crisis. What crisis? All the neighbors called to report fire POURING OUT of the church building! That's what I'm talking about!

After Jesus rose, He sent the disciples to Jerusalem to wait for the power of the Spirit to fall. They did not hold a planning meeting. They did not hold a committee meeting on church growth or study the local demographics. They waited and prayed – until the Spirit was poured out in power. And when He did, the disciples went out and turned the world upside down.

Their message was not "Ten steps to a more fulfilled life" or any such worldly tripe. It was, "Repent. Turn to the Living God. Serve Jesus. Receive the Spirit. Christ is coming back."

As I look through the entire Word of God, I do not ever see God's people changed by hearing nice words, or planning something fun, or studying population statistics. It was only when they were confronted with their desperate need for healing, for hope and for God, for truth and for holiness.

Josiah was a young king who knew little about the God of his fathers. But they found "The Book" buried in the vast halls of the Temple. He had it read to him, and he wept, tore his clothes, and swept through Israel like a holy hurricane tearing down demon altars and killing its messengers.

The Book was read to the returning exiles from Babylon, and they wept sore. But rejoice, he told them – you've come home.

But we have it reversed. We rejoice but we have not wept. We party for Jesus but we have never mourned. If God is near to the broken hearted, where does that put us? "Joy comes in the morning" – after a night of weeping!

I long for the Word of the Lord that is so rare today.

I must speak a little of one of my two remaining spiritual fathers. (The first, David Malkin, gave me the straight-up Gospel – the kind that made me weep and brought me to the cross – thank you David) The other is Rick Howard. I had met him through a friend in 1977. I spoke at his church. But the first time I sat under his message, I was riveted. Every word cut me to the quick. It was NOT pretty. It gave me no warm fuzzies. It challenged me for more of Jesus in every area of my heart and life. It showed me my lack, and His supply. God, I prayed, make my word like THAT word. And so it has been. As far as I know, I have never preached a "pink cloud" message, and by His grace, I never will.

The spiritual nature of God's people is that we tend toward spiritual deterioration. You know that about yourself. Don't you? You know we have to fight to stay fit, to stay strong, to grow, That is why "nice" messages are so dangerous – like junk food – all sugar, quick high, no nutrition. We need to be forever challenged toward MORE. My yearly fear is that on January 1st of next year, I will be exactly the same as January 1st of this year.

We need to pray for the church, for our pastors, for a fiery visitation of the Spirit of God that produces a fiery Word that will bring fiery revelation. A revelation of such overwhelming power that we will be transformed into flames of fire that will once more turn the world upside down.

"The Bible was written in tears and to tears it will yield its best treasures. God has nothing to say to the frivolous man. The whole Christian family stands in need of a restoration of penitence, humility and tears. May God send them soon." – A.W. Tozer

12 DEFENDING A FIELD

Sometimes the fight is overwhelming. And I can tell you from personal experience that sometimes the battle gets so brutal and drags on so long, that it is possible to lose all sense of it - to begin to forget why you are fighting and what the war is for. It is then that you must stand the strongest, though every ounce of you is screaming, "Stop!"

It is good when the battle lines are clear, the goals are precise and the troops are strong and ready to march. But most of this happens before one shot is fired or one sword of battle is drawn. God gives you a plan. You know your enemy. You prepare with the Word, prayer, support from fellow warriors, companions and those who send and supply you.

But the test is always on the front line. There, all romance about the glory of war disappears. There is real pain and real suffering and there are real casualties.

Did you happen to see the movie Pearl Harbor? The first part portrayed the carefree confidence of young soldiers and nurses who had not yet tasted war.

Let me be honest. Many "ministries" and churches are like that. They are safe. They are supported well, pleasing to others and full of busy activities. And all this is fine. But it isn't war.

I read about a ministry recently whose mission is leading people to Jesus through weight lifting feats. And that's great. Like Paul, I say, "As long as Christ is preached." But hearing that the ministry head filed a $500,000 tax return last year (minus perks) kind of made me sick. That's a lot of "ministry money" for doing something you like, something you're good at anyway.

But it isn't war. It's playing on the Hawaiian Islands while our brethren around the world are being slaughtered - literally.

Pearl Harbor part two: The war comes to us. And the movie was relentlessly brutal in showing what it was like - it was gory, ugly, horrific, devastating. And we were not prepared.

Well, back to my point.

Real spiritual war is hell. And no, not everyone is called to the front lines. But much of what I see isn't even IN the real war. It's G.I. Joe play-war. While mega-ministries awash in cash and good feelings play, hundreds of thousands of real men and women of God are fighting to hang on to what they have. They are working with the hardest - the worst kind of people in our eyes: Gangs. Gays. Drug addicts. Domestic violence victims. Sexually abused children. Occultists. The demon possessed. Punkers, prostitutes, prisoners. The ones many would rather not acknowledge or welcome, much less minister to.

To these warriors, and every Christian who understands the real battle we are in, I want to write this to encourage you in the fight.

Please don't think it a shallow analogy between Pearl Harbor and the Christian fight. The Christian battle is in fact more real and significant than any human war because the stakes are eternal.

I can never remember a time when I have seen genuine believers who are committed to Jesus and His Kingdom so embattled. Once clear callings and purposes have been overwhelmed by crises, illness, attacks, failures, family struggles - as well as indefinable attacks - strange confusion, spiritual lethargy, doubts and fears, uncertainty in direction and purpose and calling. Some, who have never had an unkind word said about them, have awakened to find their character, their motives and their very calling on trial by believers who unexplainably turned adversarial in an almost demonic way to assassinate their very spiritual character.

"Beloved, think it not strange concerning the fiery trial which is to try you..." (1 Peter 4:12)

If you are walking through these things, Peter says rejoice! And though it seems strange, it is not. You are no longer back home singing about the glories of war. You are in it, and you realize it is not a game. You now understand that Satan is very real, and he hates you passionately. He is throwing everything at you to kill you and take you out - lies, gossip, doubt, failure, temptation - everything.

In this moment you must not falter, even though you are not even sure why you are at war anymore. This isn't uncommon even in human battles:

When a soldier fights, he is not usually thinking, "I'm doing this for my country." He is thinking, "Kill or be killed." A soldier's instinct is survival first. The purpose for the fight is not usually upfront when the bullets are flying.

When you have been set to defend a territory - when you have been commissioned to a ministry, a mission or a call - when you have determined to stand and be 100% committed to Jesus no matter what the cost - you will enrage the enemy, and he will contest your every move, even your most insignificant move.

But, you say, "I'm not warrior! I'm not running a 'big ministry'! I'm just a Christian trying to hang on! Why is he attacking ME so hard???"

Beloved, hear me - every and any believer who stands uncompromisingly determined to live for Jesus IS a warrior. Right now believers are falling in multitudes to sin, compromise and even surrender. That makes every believer who refuses to quit a bigger, clearer target. We are in an hour where every believer must understand their vital place, take that place, keep that place, DEFEND that place!

As I said in my book on Nehemiah, the devil doesn't care how pretty or how ugly or how good or how desolate your spiritual square inch of land is. He just wants you to move, that's all! Because it used to be HIS turf! HIS land! But when you surrendered your life to Jesus, you became GOD'S property and became a hated enemy of Satan, who is determined to do everything he can to seize you back, or failing to, render you USELESS!

So now here you stand: You are weary beyond words. Once certain goals are now unclear. Once clear vision is now cloudy, as the sheer sweat of battle blinds and stings and blurs your eyes. You are tired of fighting; you are tired of LOSING. You are tired of not knowing even WHY you are fighting anymore.

There is a small passage in the Old Testament that is a perfect picture of this very place to me: "And after him was Shammah...the Philistines had gathered together into a troop where there was a piece of ground full of lentils. So the people fled...but he stationed himself in the middle of the field, defended it and killed the Philistines. So the Lord brought about a great victory." (2 Samuel 23:11-12)

Do you think the field of lentils was a big prize? No! It was a symbol of the center of the battle. We are not told why the enemy gathered in it nor why Shammah fought for it; but it's safe to assume, in Shammah's heart, he thought, "This is GOD'S land, not the Philistines'! And I'm going to wipe the enemy off of it!" And so he did. God always loves impossible odds, impossible battles waged against insurmountable enemies through unlikely heroes and unremarkable warriors! Shammah was one. His name has dual meanings: Ruin, or astonishment; desolate, or wonderful thing. The field of lentils was where he would be proven to be one or the other. And he became an astonishing warrior who did a wonderful thing: he beat the enemy through the mighty power of God! All because he simply took the center of the battle, stood, fought and refused to surrender. "...And having done all, to stand." (Ephesians 6:13b)

Your territory - your battleground - your ministry, your calling, your life - may seem as insignificant to you as a field of beans. But not to God! To Him it is the very holy ground where warriors are made, saints are proven and the devil can once again be beaten senselessly into the dust by the children of God. You don't have to know the whys of the attack, nor have complete clarity and vision. Just know that HE set you where you are at this very moment, at this very place. Remember that if your place and your life were not of infinite value and crucial importance to the God of heaven and His plan, there would be no battle raging - the mere ferocity of the fight says that this place you are defending is so important that Satan cannot let you win! That is why you MUST hold the ground. Hold it and destroy the enemy that has sought to take God's ground - because it is GOD'S GROUND! Take courage, saint - the victory is ASSURED - if only you stand!

13 GOOD GRIEF

This last year, a number of people I know and love have lost someone dear to them. The last several years have found me bereaved more times than in my entire life. Each Christmas, cards sent mean some will be answered with sad news of a friend's passing. As a human being and friend, it has been pain shared. As a minister, it is a painful challenge, knowing the call to comfort, the difficulty of doing so while still walking through my own losses.

Death is a mystery. Anyone who says otherwise probably hasn't lost anyone. Death is also an enemy; it is the result of the fall. It is human separation. And no matter how assured we are of life eternal, no one can bypass grief – or, they do so at the risk of destroying their health, their relationships and their purpose. You MUST grieve. And we of faith should NEVER minimize, deny or disparage that necessary healing.

How long does grief take?

As long as it takes.

And that is different for everyone. In the death of a terminally ill loved one, spanning months and perhaps years, the grieving often begins when the prognosis is given. A loved one with Alzheimer's forces the grieving, as the loved one goes from them before the body follows.

Sudden or traumatic death is itself like a terrible car wreck for those left behind – unexpected, it devastates their known familiar world. Denial is stronger, confusion and disorientation deeper, and jolting shocks of excruciating pain more sickening. They were just here; I touched them. They're gone. There IS no neat, palm-pilot scheduled grieving process for that kind of loss. It is a monster rollercoaster, plunging you into terrifying darkness, often followed by unexplained, almost giddy happiness, leading you to falsely believe you are "over it" – followed by another, even deeper terrifying plunge into the depths of despair.
And yes, eventually, the rollercoaster does begin to level out. But even then, there may be unexpected returns to the stomach-churning declines.

All this is – well, NORMAL! And I am frankly put off by those who try to short-circuit this painful passage for their grieving friends, pressing a time limit, singing happy tunes to the bereaved (Proverbs 25:20) or subtly condescending when they express ongoing grief – as if grieving after a certain time was an act of unbelief, some kind of unthankfulness that their loved ones are "happy with Jesus," or that the person is not "getting on with their life." (What does THAT mean? Get on with your amputated leg?)

Grieving is as complex as each individual's relationship to the lost loved one. I have a dear friend whose father died in December. His father left his family when my friend was ten, went on to have two other families, leaving a trail of carnage, abuse and alcoholic destruction everywhere he went.

My friend had tried to stay in touch with his father, tried vainly to make his dad be a dad to him. He never did. He had not the capacity. He liked his son; but he had no capacity to engage him, love him, father him.

When his father was diagnosed inoperable, he went to him, he loved him, let him know he was forgiven. He died a Christian.

But my friend said, "I've been grieving him my whole life."

I was a pallbearer. I watched my friend weep five minutes before we entered the cemetery, and as he said goodbye for the last time.

Then nothing, until a month later, a song triggered the loss, and he wept again.

Piecemeal grief is his cross. And I will bear it with him, for as long as it takes, without recrimination, or weariness, or questions, or demands that he "move on". As my cousin said about the death of her mother, and my dad, "The pain changes." It does not go away – not in this life.

And isn't it right that it is so? A two day mourning, then "on with the show" – what does that say? It devalues the lost one's place of love and importance in our lives. Doesn't it? And a fine act of denial short grieving is at that.

Let me simplify it. A father goes to war. Should the wife and child and parents not weep, not long, not hurt, not GRIEVE? Yes, they (hopefully) will return alive. But oh, how they will be missed!

And what of a missionary who departs, making it clear they will not return?

Should we shun tears, be happy they are "going with Jesus," then "get on with it"?

Certainly not!

Our grief – and I daresay, the depth of our grief, is the measure of the value of the love we held for the one who leaves.

Why, then, are we so quick to force others – perhaps ourselves – to "get over it," not cry, not grieve?

We're trying to scare the death mask away, or deny its very existence at all. "It's not there; I won't face it. Stop talking about it, life goes on..."

But we will ALL face this – perhaps many times. The least we can do is to provide comfort, non-judgmental silence, and a wide berth for those in the awful shock of the empty heart. As one writer said, "We are all in the same ship on a stormy sea, and we owe each other a terrible loyalty."

Don't we?

Today's brittle response to another's grief will be your bitter education tomorrow.

I know, I am partial to defending the grieving. As a soldier is partial to his comrades in battle. Don't fault me for that. Someday, everyone will understand my meaning.

For those who comfort those who mourn, I offer these simple guides:

1. Set no time limit on grief. Everyone must grieve according to the depth, lack of depth, or unfinished business of their relationship to those they have lost.

2. Words are not very helpful. An arm, a hand, a call, a walk, a gift, a hug, a tear: these are the most powerful messages.

3. Most believers know the scriptures on death. If you quote them, do so when asked or needed, not when you feel the need to "admonish" them for grieving.

4. Don't wait for the other person to talk about it. After a few months, they already feel burdensome about "still grieving." Step out; ask, "How are you doing with your loss?" They will be so thankful you cared enough to

ask, to recognize they are not "over it" yet.

For the lonely pilgrim on this path, I offer this, and this from my still mending heart:

1. Take as long as you need. No one but God has a right to set a limit on your grief. Lovingly separate yourself from those who don't get it and simply make you feel more alone.

2. Set your own limits. Grief MUST be walked out. Usually, your own breaking heart demands, forces you to stop and heal. But be careful not to allow grief to fall into morbid contemplation. Your loved one is dead; you are not. You MUST not die with them – not in actuality, not in disconnection from life, not in affection with others. Grief at first will consume all – your time, your life, your heart. But then, you must act. They are GONE. You cannot change it, and you must not die. Take time to grieve – but then, say, "Now I must take time to live." You will grieve to some degree until heaven. But you must not cease to live.

Finally, loved one, remember this – death, the enemy – the separation – is but for a moment. We do not mourn as those who have no hope. (1 Thess. 4:13) But we DO mourn. God will never deny us that. But your loved one lived, and is alive still with Him. And one day, you will know the sweet embrace that will wipe away a million tears – when you come Home, and see your beloved shining, running to your arms.

And then, you will grieve no more.

This is our promise. It is our hope. It is the balm that in time, mends the pain.

14 THE BLANK PAGE

When I'm in church, something happens there that doesn't happen in any other setting. It must be the combination of worship, communion, fellowship and teaching. My mind and heart kick into high gear. I'm thinking thoughts I've never had, solving problems I couldn't fix before and finding new vision and new ways to carry out my call. I understand why the Scriptures tell us not to forsake gathering together. We need fellowship, in a million ways and for a million reasons. There are things I receive alone with God I can never get out of church; but there are things I get in church I can never get alone. It's a marvelous gift, a mystery of the "communion of saints" – here, now.

For this reason, I'm glad for my church. And specifically, for my church bulletin, because the pastor always has an outline with lots of space for notes – and often the back of the outline is completely blank.

That leaves a ton of space for notes, ideas, sudden words from God. And sometimes, room for kids to write me a question about the message. Or something I said in class. Or just doodles. (We are paying attention, Pastor, I promise!)

A few Sundays ago, it was an especially busy Sunday and the bulletin was packed. Suddenly I got an important idea and I had to write it down before I forgot it. So I rummaged through the book-sized bulletin, and – NOTHING! No paper! No space! I nearly panicked. Then I realized I could use my palm pilot, and promptly wrote the idea down on the palm of my hand. (Well, it's a low-income palm pilot.)

Then I heard the still, small Voice of the Holy Spirit: "Don't let anyone or anything fill up the blank page of your life that I wish to write upon."

Sometimes I've been asked how I've kept the "fire" alive, the passion for Jesus, for 33 years. Grace, for one; I'm ornery, for another. As I started to think about it, I realized one of the center points has been this: Knowing that Jesus is alive, I endeavor to start each day with Him, offering Him the blank page of my day, and my life. Sometimes I have to fight hard for that, especially when I travel. But when I am home, it's the most important thing

I can do. If I do, the day seems ordered and peaceful; if I don't, it's chaotic and troubling. As one person said, if you get the first hole wrong when you button up a shirt, you'll never get the rest of it right.

That precious first moments of my day are the blank page of my life. I've come to anticipate it like a child waiting to open presents on Christmas morning. I expect God to meet me. I anticipate His friendship. I listen to Him speak. He begins to write on my blank page. Suddenly, I'm filled with an awesome sense that anything could happen, that breakthroughs and miracles are at hand, and that my life isn't being concluded but it is just beginning!

David, reflecting on life, said, "We finish our years like a sigh." The cry on my heart is, "Not with a sigh, Lord – but with a shout! With a battle-cry!" I want to be so engaged in the life God gave me that when I arrive, angels will have to pry the sword from my hand!

Jesus is the same yesterday, today and forever. When I pick up His Word each day and let Him begin to write on the blank page of my life, there's no longing for "The good old days." No regrets of "what might have been." Rather, the battles of David are today; and the warnings of Saul's failure. The Acts of the Apostles are MY goals; the prophecies of all prophets speak to MY life, NOW.

Oh, how this Blank Page time is contested! My mind wanders. The phone rings incessantly. The rush and crush of the day looms. But I SEIZE this gift and let these moments be my sail.

It extends beyond as well, for God continues to write throughout the day. But the contest for the pen continues, too. Two things personally threaten to fill my blank page.

One, the Tyranny of Things. Although I have twice in my life lost all my material possessions, somehow it's all come back! Clutter is the enemy of my mind and spirit. Technology makes it worse. E mail clutter. Mailing lists, cell phone lists, junk mail, magazines, 200 channels of television to choose from and six different ways of recording them...all of it tries to write confusion on my Page. I have been in the process of unsubscribing to almost every magazine, throwing away junk mail and "wish books" before even looking at them, and giving away several boxes of things a month. I have pared down my TV time to a bare minimum. As my house and mind are cleared, He once again finds quietness to write.

The other threat for me is volunteerism.

I want to be very careful here, because I believe in the purposes of God's work, the need for workers and the necessity of laborers in the Harvest. And frankly, too many would rather not help with anything if they could get away with it.

But in an age where "making a difference" and "finding your purpose" are the buzzwords of the hour, we have forgotten that our FIRST priority is to love and be with Jesus. Everything else should flow from that. Otherwise, we're just doing things for God to avoid the aching void of our empty spirits. I saw a bumper sticker that was awful, yet it spoke to me. It said, "Jesus is coming back. Look busy." And I wonder how much of our spiritual, Martha-like busy work is like that: He's coming; I better have something going here so I can look good.

As a reluctant "professional volunteer" that usually says yes without thinking or praying, a word of caution: If Satan can't get you to do one bad thing, he will get you to do a hundred good things that aren't God's things, that God didn't authorize you to do, so your blank page is too full for God to write on. And in some churches, once you're known for volunteering for one thing, watch out! You'll be asked to volunteer for everything, and you will have a terrible time saying no as the snowball accumulates, gains momentum and eats up even the time reserved for Jesus alone.

I have had to learn to say no unless it is an obvious need I must fill, or God gives me His okay. I have learned the hard way that just because there is a need, does not mean I am supposed to fill it. Mary demanded Jesus fix the wedding wine crisis right away. Jesus did it when His time was right. Mary and Martha cried for Jesus to come and heal Lazarus. Jesus let him die – because the plan was for resurrection, not healing. How many blessings do we miss because we do not listen, do not wait, we rush ahead trying to "be busy" without really knowing what HE wants? Jesus said He only did what He saw the Father do. Wouldn't we be wise to do the same?

Take the blank page of your life before the Father every day. Guard that page jealously, and let Him begin to speak to you, love and strengthen you, and write HIS will and purpose for your life. You are His workmanship – His "poeima" – let Him have all the time and the attention He needs to write with beauty and strength. Deny the distractions, clean house of the things mental and material that sap you, chain you, keep you cluttered, and let Him fill your house with HIS treasure.

Your first priority is to be with Him – and as you give Him your blank page, He will write an eternal song with everything you say and do.

15 LIFE IS IN THE MOMENTS

Most of us believe that life is some kind of linear journey from birth to death – point A to point B. In one way that is true. Paul spoke of finishing his race. We are called to be sojourners, looking for a Heavenly City which is to come.

But our world is so bent on success, goals, getting ahead, investing, etc., that most of us – even believers – miss a very important truth; Life is in the Moments.

I understand that there are two words for time in the New Testament: Chronos and Kairos. Chronos, from where we derive the word "chronology" refers to linear time. Clocks. Point A to Point B. Calendars. "The clock is running."

Kairos is the moment that the Eternal slices right into our linear time and is present –and time stops. God speaks. History is changed. It is when the Eternal invades the linear and we know we are not – nor ever have been – alone.

We do so much to avoid the inevitable conclusion of our linear prison. Men and women have affairs to turn back the clock and "recapture" their adolescence. Stars and fading socialites fill their faces with Botox, scare the gray away with dyes, try to stay "cool" with kids half their age. We accumulate things, strive for better positions, better houses, better cars…

…all to avoid the inevitable. Our linear time has an end. So much of all we do is whistling in the dark, ignoring our fear of what the end will be.

The scriptures are clear about linear time: "Teach us to number our days, that we may apply our hearts to wisdom."(Psalm 90:12)

But how do we live in the light of this inevitability?

We come to see that life is in the moments.

I have so many snapshots of the Eternal invading my linear life. There was a warm southwest afternoon in 1976 when I first moved to El Paso when we fellowshipped and sang all afternoon at Madeline Park, watching billowy white thunderclouds lazily gathering, feeling the balmy breeze…walking down a pecan tree lined road with a best friend, feeling the veneer between heaven and earth was so thin that we could almost touch the wings of angels…and we turned a corner, and the Eternal moment was tangibly gone…

…The one and only time I was "drunk" in the Spirit, sitting in a corner of a house fellowship, awash in worship, overcome by a love and Presence so strong that I could only sit in the corner and grin, not even able to get up on my own…

…the moment, two months before my father died, as he sat and held my hand on the couch in the dying dusk, telling me how much he loved me, that I had been like an angel to him…

No, I no longer count my linear days by achievements, speaking tours or invitations. I count them by these Eternal moments, when time stops and God joins the moment to speak, to love, to engage my life in friendship and Grace.

I felt Him there in the Thanksgiving day a few years ago when a young friend, without a place to go that day, spent the day with me at Denny's, then in the park where we made "leaf angels" in the crunchy Mulberry carpet…

…I felt Him with me in St Louis in September with my friends Tony, Mary Jo & Claire, laughing so hard I hurt…reminded of the preciousness of true friends in battle…

I felt him in the embrace of my adopted grandson as I was leaving last week, and he would not let me go, snuggling into my neck like an eternal blanket of Father's love.

Do you know what I am talking about?

"If only you had known the time of your visitation." (Luke 19:44)

Jesus came to His own, and His own did not receive Him. Kairos invaded Chronos – a moment they had anticipated, waited for – and they missed it. Why?

They were too busy running religious affairs. Their pride resisted Messiah's humble form. He simply wasn't what they expected – or wanted. So they resented the beauty of His story of the lilies, because it confronted their greed and accumulation. They were shocked at His embracing of children, because their intellectual elitism did not bow to lesser minds. They despised His lavish forgiveness of the prostitute and the tax gatherer because they worked so hard to be perfect – and better than the gentile dogs and filthy sinners.

For this, He wept. They missed the moment because of their selfish, prideful expectations of what their Messiah should look like and what He should do. But, as one writer said, He comes in some distressing disguises.

But what about us? God intersects our linear life – every day. But we're too busy to see Him, too stressed to listen for Him, too numb to feel Him when He comes.

Many believers have stopped expecting Him altogether because He does not come when we expected. "Lord, if You had been there, my brother would not have died." "We thought that He was the one who was to come." "Are you He, or should we look for another?"

Two disciples were on the road to Emmaus; they were so overcome with grief and disappointment, so preoccupied with thoughts of their now uncertain future, they did not even recognize Jesus when He joined them. But in the simple joy and comfort of breaking bread with their newfound friend, they saw Jesus – and realized He had been there all the time! Life IS in the moments! But we must be looking, hearing, expecting Him in the simple, the distressful, the painful, the ordinary moments of every day.

What about you, dear friend? Has your quest for more, fear for tomorrow, regret over the past dulled your hearing? Has your frenzied Martha-like serving and drive to "do more for God" denied you what really matters – sitting at His feet, just listening, just being with the Savior?

For many, it is the struggle with dashed hopes, broken dreams, personal failure and feeling God is not who we thought, did not answer our prayer as we wanted or needed. And some give up hope for Him to ever come through again.

To you, He says, "Blessed are they who are not offended in Me." Disappointments, betrayals, shattered dreams, sudden devastating losses…they come to ALL. The pivotal moment comes when we say,

"Father, YOU are in this moment. Even THIS You will turn for good." And then you will see Him there – the Kairos intersecting th Chronos – weaving even THIS into His loving plan.

Friends, my life has been a wild rollercoaster of great opportunities, dashed dreams, caring friends, brutal betrayal, awesome promise and crushed hopes and plans. I have been blessed with precious ministry in extraordinary places, and faced exile from all I knew and loved. In five years, I have seen nearly all of my mentors, family and many loved friends gone to be with Jesus.

Am I offended? Offended that my life never reached stellar heights, never saw publication, never spoke to tens of thousands of kids? At times I was disappointed. Heartbroken, in fact. At times I felt the losses would never end.

But through it all, I can say that God gave me little of what I wanted, ALL that I needed, and more than I ever dared to ask for. What else does anyone need, really?

I feel His Kairos still in every ministry opportunity, every unexpected open door and breakthrough.

But I am learning to live in the adventure of the everyday moments He is near – in every precious page of scripture taken in – in every time of worship at church – but also in tonight's spectacular sunset after a day of refreshing rain – in a call from my loved cousin or brother – in the privilege of a good cup of coffee in the early morning crisp air.

In the rush of serving and living, dear one, don't miss the embrace of your mate, the laughter of your children, the awesome freedom to worship we have, and a thousand other moments when He is Present – because those moments pass and they may never come again. Every day is a gift wrapped in grace to be opened by the child of heart who knows all good gifts come from His hand, and He longs for the joy of being there to see you open them.

Life – God – truly IS in the moments.

16 PROPPED UP

"The battle increased that day, and the King of Israel propped himself up in his chariot facing the Syrians until evening; and about the time of sunset, he died." – 2 Chronicles 18:33-34

I have lived to see the church of Jesus shining and full of His glory. I have been on the streets and seen famous men like David Wilkerson and his wife Gwen humbly praying and loving the street people of the Tenderloin in San Francisco, bringing God's grace and healing to drug addicts, the homeless, the criminals and prostitutes. I lived in the days of the great Kathryn Kuhlman, who did not think herself anything, but whose frail body was yielded as a vessel for the mighty Holy Spirit to flow through. I witnessed the sea of young people blanketing the beaches of Southern California awaiting baptism. I have stood in a crowd of thousands, all with faces lifted and hands raised in adoration of Jesus while the anointed singers of God – Keith Green, Chuck Girard, 2nd Chapter of Acts – freely gave of their hearts and lives to bring us into His presence.

I have sat cross-legged at the altar of a church, a young boy bleeding and rejected and lost, head in my hands, and felt the gentle hands of a 60 year old pastor on my head, as he prayed, and wept over me…

I came under the care of, as she called herself, "a fat little Polish-Irish mama" named Audrey Meier, who although she was world renowned for her powerful songs, including "To Be Used of God" and "His Name is Wonderful" took me into her heart and gave me an anchor in my first troubled days of ministry.

I was bonded to a man of God, Rick Howard, who reached out to a young, and untamed, untrained wild stallion and saw my potential – and dare I say it? God's anointing – and gave me his support, his pulpit occasionally, and his life experience, father to son, shared over meals, calls and walks down the streets of Redwood City and San Francisco.

Now that I am reaching a zenith of sorts, though not yet at twilight and with Caleb's spirit and not the spirit of the giant-fearing spies, I look back and find myself grateful for what I had, sad for the loss of many of these things and people, and genuinely frightened for the future of the western church, and for this generation. For we have lost the stuff that makes the church the church, God's people strong and unafraid, and the next generation secure and full of vision and fire.

The Western Church has become a compromised Ahab, going to war for self's sake, and ending up a propped-up mess in the throes of spiritual death.

I was not there for the beginnings of Graham, Roberts, Kuhlman, Wilkerson and others. But I was the recipient of their fruit and their faithfulness. I was a partaker in the great West Coast outpouring that came by no man's hand but through the faithful prayers of hidden saints crying for revival, and resulted in an astonishing flash flood of miracles, salvations, healings and lives changed forever.

So what happened? How did the church go from life-changers to life-improvers and life-coaches? How did we become a propped-up caricature of the glorious bride of Christ and become a mockery because of our excess, our sins, our silliness and our lack of substance? And how do we "strengthen the things which remain" into one final battle battalion that will deal Satan one last deadly blow before we go Home? For I will not write of what was, nor bemoan what is, without giving hope – and a plan – to regain what we have lost to selfishness and pride. There WILL be a remnant, of that I am sure. All my heart is determined to help to raise it up.

In studying the Kings of Israel and Judah, it is always saddening and maddening to hear of kings who ALMOST got it right, but who allowed some compromise, or neglect, or bad relationships, or excesses, or deception to mar their record. How like them we are! How did we get here?

It's the little foxes that spoiled the vine, and that still do.

The Jesus movement fell prey to three things: Unresolved sin issues in much of the young leadership, the commercializing of the Holy Spirit, and the controlling of the people. Leaders who did not deal with sin became either monster wolves like David Berg of the Children of God, or simply fell prey to sin and were no more.

Then, Christian & secular businesses turned the Jesus Movement - and its followers - into a commodity. Jesus Junk (remember doggie witness t-shirts?) added the pockets of the greedy, and recording artists joined the limelight with the secular rich and famous, with rare exceptions such as

Keith Green and Rich Mullins, who refused to sell out the Gospel for thirty pieces of silver.

Then, with good intentions, a group of older Florida men rose up with the "Shepherding Movement" and first sweet-talked, then cajoled, and eventually BEAT much of the Jesus movement into submission. To them.

It became a spiritual bloodbath. The damage is still being felt. (Most of these men, thankfully, have repented.)

The Charismatic movement began to be corrupted by prosperity extremes, deliverance madness and a form of entitlement that led to many leaders falling into public sin, going into biblical error, and making a laughingstock out of the church.

Despite pockets of genuine revival, within a couple of decades, most of what the Spirit had done was a shadow memory, replaced by the logical outcome of unchecked excess, loss of missionary vision and leaning on the arm of the flesh: The MegaChurch. Church as Corporation. Pastors as executives, people as product and "plug-ins" connecting to the church Mainframe. Large numbers and big growth via the dumbing-down of the Gospel, diluting the message of sin, the cross and repentance, in favor of Your Best Life Now, endless series of humanistic help with scripture tags added, and the delusion that by making the church like a big social club minus anything about God that is TOO offensive, we would make disciples. We didn't. We just swelled our ranks and made ourselves fat and useless toward real discipleship and evangelism.

Youth ministry especially suffered – the ministry that is SO vital to our future – as it became professional babysitting, entertainment, games and more games, a rave without the drugs, and youth pastors moving on as quickly as they were settled in, looking for a better-paying gig as a REAL pastor somewhere. Gone was all teaching on the spiritual warfare we face. Scarce was the Word of God. Gone were youth Pastors – replaced by youth DIRECTORS who were expected to herd cattle, not feed sheep.

An alienated, disaffected and disconnected generation rejected it all – the excess, the shallowness, and the glitz and hype of the Crystal Cathedral era of the Western Church, and exchanged it for a quest for something REAL.

That quest placed them right into the waiting clutches of the theological wolves and deceived socialist teachers who created the "emergent movement"; a new village filled with uncertainty, doubt, murky theology and spiritual cloud castles that have little substance in truth. Worship is now being exchanged for secular music, the cross for a coffee cup, communion for a quick Jesus snack and the Word for worthless questioning of God's truth.

In the meantime, the Megas keep propping themselves up in the chariot, not realizing the battle has turned bad, and the emergent is singing protest songs and swilling beer and smoking cigars and Hookahs, celebrating their "freedom in Christ" in the passenger seat.

The wheels are coming off the Mega chariot.

We have become a propped-up caricature of what we were, of what Jesus called us to be. We have the form of godliness but deny its power; we have the framework of church but little of the substance or heart; we're VERY busy, but merely being frantic so we don't stop and realize it's just motion for the sake of it, whistling in the gathering dark.

But God will not leave us without hope, without a remnant. All throughout Israel and Judah's history, no matter how dark, God raised up men and women of God, many of them young, to raise the standard of truth, tear down the idols of Baal and Ashtoreth, pronounce the Word of God against the leaders that compromised, and shocked and forced the people to decide who they would serve.

In every place I've gone, in every place I've preached this last few years, I have seen a growing number of young people hungrily devour every measure of truth given to them. They are tired of the compromise. They are sickened by the games and troubled by the lack of direction. They want more. They want REAL purpose. They want real direction. They want real relationship with Jesus, and not the sweet socialist Marxist Gandhi prototype put forth by the Mergents, but the One who turned over the moneychangers' tables, loved the prostitute and outcast, spoke shattering truth without one care for offending or "alienating the unchurched"; they want the Lamb-Lion who spoke tough words, proved His love by letting them slaughter Him, and promised He would never leave them. They want the Lord who is not vague but told us exactly who He is, what He wants and how to live valiantly, deliberately and unashamed of the ONLY message that can save – Christ Jesus and Him crucified.

I believe God wants to raise up a generation of youth, but also of old War Vets who knew the real thing, fought the real battles, bled when we gave up the war, but still have all the right tools and weapons to teach this young generation the art of War. He is going to call them out of retirement, gather a young generation to them, and give them the job of teaching them to fight well and fight to victory.

While the Ahab church, full of compromise and ungodly goals props itself up in attempt to recapture the glory days and give the appearance that all is well, God's raised-up ones will stand like David on the hill, awaiting the war against the Goliath of this age, ready to fulfill their destiny.

I hear the sound of a Shofar…

17 AT THE CROSSROADS

So many Christians are bound by a "rapture mentality" that they have consistently failed to see the wolves at the gate. It has been so for generations. I remember clearly Corrie ten Boom telling of a Chinese pastor that wept telling her, "I preached that the church would be raptured before the tribulation. Then the communists came and my people were not prepared for suffering and even death because of their faith." He could hardly live with himself.

I truly hope Jesus comes back before the tribulation, but for the suffering church worldwide, it is hardly an issue – they are already suffering in a way we cannot fathom here.

This is not about theology, but about being prepared. And we are not.

Having been a believer since 1969, there have been many times when world events were so out of control that I anxiously wondered, "Is Jesus about to return? Is this it?" He did not then, but mark my words, He WILL come. After a number of years, one learns to discern the times better. We are near. Believers who can discern the times and the intent of God for our age will be crucial in the days ahead. So I want to share with you what I see.

This was a political year, but so much more. If we had seen "beyond the veil" we would have seen a clash of angelic and demonic so savage it would have terrified us. It is bigger than the war on terror, or the economy. It is about our national soul. The only thing preventing judgment is the prayers of the believers.

One of the things we consistently heard during the campaign was, "This nation is deeply divided," That is correct. Let's talk about that.

Centuries ago, Israel too was deeply divided. A man named Elijah came to divide it right in two. In fact, he came to clarify and finalize that division. The country was so corrupt that God sent Elijah to draw the line – a dividing line: "Who is on the Lord's side?" Fire came from heaven and consumed corrupters and corrupted alike – those who chose their corruption over God Himself. Not exactly the candidate of unity, was he?

And that's where we've gotten it wrong. I constantly hear, "Jesus came to preach peace." He certainly did not. He said, "Do not think that I have come to bring peace, but a sword, For I have come to set a man against his father, a daughter against her mother....and a man's enemies will be those of his own household." (Matthew 10:34-36)

In the church's zeal to attract the world, imitate the world and not offend the world, we have lost our fire. We've forgotten that we are called to be separate – spiritual troublemakers – ones who turn the world upside down! We are called to be – dare I say it? Dividers. Dividing truth from lie, reality from fantasy, righteousness from sin and corruption. Who we are are, what we believe, who we belong to will put us in direct opposition to the spirit of this age, the antichrist spirit. Get used to it. It's about to get a lot worse.

But, you say, aren't we supposed to love people and bring them to Jesus? Of course. But we aren't a tourist bureau. "Come to the Kingdom – great views, great food, friendly people!"

No. Better to see it as a house on fire while people sleep. You don't knock and say, "Sorry to bother, but, uh, come over to our house – it's not on fire. And we LOVE you!"

No, love dictates that we use any and all means to wake people up and get them OUT of the burning house! Don't ask firefighters to be polite. And don't ask a true Christian to be inoffensive. The cross, Paul said, is an offense to those who are perishing.

In these last days, people will be saved not because they find it fun but because they find it a matter of life or death.

(Note: The following italicized paragraphs were written three elections ago; it is chilling to see how much closer we are now to what is in this article):

This was a year that was politically divided – and decided – by the Christian vote. I was taken aback. All my years I've seen elections come and go and Christians largely took an, "It doesn't matter, Jesus is coming back" attitude. I guess we finally realized that while we basked away in our comfortable churches, the devil had been taking our most precious liberties, our beliefs, and our children. This year it got serious. The ten commandments were banned from public places. People were demanding the right to have a doctor pull a 2nd trimester baby from the womb, jam a metal tube into its brain and suck its life out. (It's called partial birth abortion.) And to top it all, gays were demanding marriage rights and some courts gave it to them. In one year, Satan moved his three favorite issues to the front of the line – the elimination of God's law, the slaughter of babies (infant sacrifice, like the old testament) and the destruction of sexual wholeness for our children.

Perhaps Christians heard the anti-God, antichrist rhetoric and began to see the handwriting on the wall. Perhaps some remembered Nazi Germany, where Christians largely did NOTHING until it was too late. Perhaps they saw into the future, and realized that if we did not act, our future liberty to preach the Gospel of truth will be in danger.

In any event, Christians did respond this time. And clearly, the prevailing issue that turned the tide was neither the economy or the war. It was morality.

Almost as soon as the election ended, the angry cries began: It's the Christians who ruined this election. The "Jesus freaks", as one politician and several activists called us. Michael Moore blamed "Jesus Land." If you are too dull to detect the demonic venom in these reactions, you are in real trouble.

There is a backlash coming. Take advantage of the next 4 years to do everything possible to further the Kingdom of God. The storm is gathering in wicked human hearts, and before it is over, a raw hatred for believers will explode and rage to destroy those who will stand for truth, cost what it may.

And this is where we are at the crossroads. It has been easier to be a Christian in this country than anywhere on earth in history. Think about that. We go to church when and where we want, talk to people about the Lord without going to jail or being beheaded. In former bastions of liberty like Europe and Canada, anti-Semitism and persecution for believers are forcing Christians to count the cost of true discipleship. Europe, in fact, is very much shaping up to be the antichrist government we once envisioned only in last days books and movies. The fiction is becoming fact – fast. Even the EU financial system has been given a chilling name – OCCULT.

What does that have to do with us in the States? The tide will begin to rise against believers. We believe in the good news of Jesus; but if you read the book of Acts, repentance was preached. In addition, idolatry and sorcery were opposed and immorality decried. Paul opposed a sorcerer and he went blind! Not exactly our modern version of "friendship evangelism."

The crossroads we face is a crisis of the Word of God, the holy Scriptures.

It is time to get past "devotional reading" and seize the Word of God for revolutionary LIVING. It is time to stop treating the scriptures like a comforting pillow and take it up as a life transforming sword.

The other day I was attempting to eat a pomegranate that had sat too long. As I cracked it open, I found half of it was ripe and half was rot. If any of it was to be edible, the rotten half had to be cut away and discarded. If I had not done it then, the rotted half would have quickly infected and destroyed the healthy fruit.

In a moment, I saw the church. For the sake of "unity" we have kept the church "whole." But as we have sat idle, the spiritual rot within has begun to infect the whole. Believers standing for corrupt moral-political spokespeople, the pursuit of prosperity rather than godliness, the softening and watering down of the offensive message of the cross in order to be "seeker friendly" – and worse – the publication of corrupted versions of the scripture such as "Good As New" to accommodate licentious lifestyles, the acceptance of occult literature as messages about God (see "Looking for God in Harry Potter"), and that which no church in history has ever dared do – ordain homosexual priests.

The devil loves a void, and he has come into our midst and sown his rot, and it is becoming a cancer to the parts of the church body that, although healthy, have been spiritually apathetic, idle, content and unused.

The Sword of Truth will be wielded to sever the corrupt from the whole – to cut off the leaven of compromise from the unleavened that remains.
Every believer must decide whether the Word of God, and the truth of it – every word – is true – and if true, to be willing to speak it, live it, and use it, to fight for the truth, cost what it may.

Because the church has idly rested, contented, avoiding the battle for our nation's future, the wolves are at the gate. Seizing on the opportunity of our sense of ease and invincibility, the devil is coming to challenge our very ability to preach the Word of God with liberty in our churches.

In Canada, you can now be charged with a hate crime for reading scriptures against homosexuality in a negative way and be jailed. Some already have.
Last week I was visiting some of our college kids at Starbucks. While standing in line, I realized there was a couple engaged in a passionate kiss right in front of me. It was two young MEN. My world spun. I went home in shock. "Where have I BEEN?" I said aloud. Then I realized the gay issue (which I have had to address more times in the last month than in the last

ten years with youth) is going to be the first volley in this war. It's as if I could hear the devil say, "Yes, just try to oppose this. You'll go to jail for this if you do." In fact, even trying to reach the gay community for Jesus is going to bring furious opposition.

It was then I realized that I had to make my own decision at this crossroads: Will I let anyone, any man or any law forbid me to preach any scripture from the Word of God? NO! A thousand times NO! If I do not have the guts to preach ALL of the Word of God, I am not fit to preach ANY of it. My decision was made: I will not be silenced. I will proclaim the truth in love, cost what I may. It may one day cost everything. So be it.

The first issue may be homosexuality, but on its heels, the time may come when anyone who speaks the truth about witchcraft, drug use, fornication or adultery will be violently opposed and perhaps charged with a hate crime. Remember, John was beheaded for opposing Herod's adulterous marriage. It may not come tomorrow. But it WILL come.

And what of these coming days for us? Israel continues to be the flashpan and focus of Biblical and prophetic human history. With the Sanhedrin reseated for the first time in nearly 2,000 years, all things point to the coming of Jesus and the fulfillment of all things written in the Book.

And how do we respond? Recently I shared my excited response concerning prophetic events with some folks – excited because even though hard times are ahead, our redemption draws near.

The response from one person downplayed all I had said, casting questions on my interpretation of prophecy, comforting everyone not to be afraid because, they said. GOD WOULD NOT LET US BE HURT BY ANYTHING. But the blood of the saints and martyrs past and present are testimony against such false security. He said He would sustain us THROUGH – not AROUND – tribulation. And, I realized, in my call to prepare believers and raise up young warriors who can stand the test, the opposition will come from within as well as without – from those frightened of suffering, from those refusing to follow the Way of the Cross, from those unwilling to give up comfortable lives to enter into the Battle of the Ages – from those who read the Word of God as pick-and-choose words of comfort (and they are comforting) rather than a manual for battle and a call to total surrender.

We are soon approaching another mount of decision where the mad prophets of Baal will face the true Elijahs of God, and all must decide:

"Who is on the Lord's side?"

At this crossroads lies the Word of God. Pick it up. Embrace it to your heart. Absorb it. And then speak it, preach it, believe it and use it – and to you will belong the strength to stand, the power of God to do miracles, the message of salvation and the Hope of Eternity,

Any other road in this hour of decision is spiritual insanity.

18 BRONZE SHIELDS FOR GOLD

God has a "gold standard." He has it for truth, for His church, for ministry and for His children.

In the days of Rehoboam, Solomon's son, the enemy had come into God's house and stolen the Gold Shields. Rehoboam replaced them with bronze ones.

There is so much to be learned through Rehoboam's short life. Solomon, his father, had deteriorated from a wise man of God to a compromised pagan idol worshipper consumed by his love of – and lust for – women. Solomon's son – like all the Kings, and all of us – started with nothing but possibilities before him. Through hundreds of years of kings – and hundreds of years of Christians – it has been the same. God lays before us an opportunity to do His will, to seek Him out, to do spectacular exploits.

He awaits our faith – our determination - our willingness to pay the price and to walk in His ways.

Rehoboam failed - spectacularly. He learned nothing from his father's mistakes. He cared little for his father's God.

At first, it looked like he might start out his reign making good decisions. He called his father's advisors and counselors together and asked them how he should rule. Their advice should be the gold standard of every pastor, youth pastor and ministry leader: "If you will be a servant to these people this day, and serve them, then they will be your servants forever." In other words, serve like Jesus did, and people will be more than willing to help you shoulder the work of the Kingdom. (1 Kings 12:1-11)

But, Rehoboam ignored their counsel. Instead he asked his childhood buddies what they thought. They told him to tell the people, "My father put a heavy burden on you. I'm going to add to it!" His arrogance split the kingdom into pieces.
I'm very concerned about the new template for youth ministry and church. Oh, I know, I'm one of the old school now…how did that happen? But my concern is not from my age, but from experience. The emergent model

goes something like this: "Hey, we appreciate all you older folks and what you did. Hey, hang around, we need mentors. But it's our time, so just try to quietly exit stage left and let us run the show now."

But that's not God's way. As a young minister, I never would have DREAMED of doing what I did without not just godly peers, but fathers and mothers in the faith. In the tough times, my peers offered me prayers and mainly, "Well, just trust God." But my mothers and fathers in Jesus gave me hard-won wisdom tried in the fire, and their ministry to me provided the backbone of all I am now.

"Teach it to your children, and your children's children…" That is God's Way. "Youth run ministry," without the net of elders will always end in arrogance, pride and shattered lives.

I heard someone talking about the need for "younger elders." I had to laugh at this ultimate oxymoron. Elders are supposed to be….ELDER.
No, wisdom does not always come with age. And I am always telling our kids about Jeremiah and Timothy and Daniel and the kids that changed the world. Even now I am watching God raise up an army of Spirit-filled, on-fire kids filled with the Word of God and His Power. There is no question that the torch will be passed to the next generation – as it should be.
My concern is that this Rehoboam generation is running a race, but no torch has been passed. They're just…running. They are sprinting for a marathon. They will burn out without marathon training and the torch being passed from battle-hardened and tested – though weary – soldiers that have gone before them. A guaranteed recipe for spiritual disaster is a Rehoboam youth ministry that only accepts its own counsel.

Because of Rehoboam's poor choices in counsel, the result was a series of more poor choices that ended in a failed reign and a divided Kingdom. Whenever we as Christian leaders take our counsel from the world, the popular and the exciting, we have abandoned the tried path in favor of the easy one. God, nevertheless, would not allow the total removal of Judah or Rehoboam. He even made allowances for Rehoboam's youth and experience.

But Shishak, king of Egypt, attacked Judah and robbed the temple. He took the gold shields Solomon had made. Rehoboam replaced them with bronze ones. So when the king came to the temple, instead of the glorious gold shields being brought out to attest to the king's glory, they brought out cheap brass ones. (1 Kings 14:25-28)

Same form of shield, but different value.

I see in this a cautionary tale for our modern church. The very scary thing about churches and ministries is that you follow certain worldly success formulas, you CAN have a successful church. The scarier part is that you can do all of that, and the Spirit of God may not even be present anymore.

Same form – different value.

There was a time – and I am witness to it – that the Spirit of God's presence and power was moving on the church, saving young lives by the thousands, healing, setting captives free and changing lives forever. That was the GOLD STANDARD that I cannot let go of or settle for less than.

But settle we did.

The thing about the Spirit of God is, He is a wind that blows where He will. He is a Cloud that MOVES, and when we get a "formula" to try to patent, expand or exploit what God is doing, He WILL move on. That is precisely why we are in such a spiritual mess now. The Jesus movement of the 1970's – good thing. But it scared leaders because there was no "control" to what the Spirit was doing. So they took control with the horrid Shepherding movement which proceeded to slaughter thousands of young believers and sent the Spirit of God packing.

Following that were a series of man-created movements, and after a generation of exchanging the Gold Shields of the Glory of God for the Bronze facsimiles of manmade religious experiences, the fruit is megachurch, seeker friendly and the Purpose Driven. Never has there been a more humanistic, corporate imitation of the Spirit of God's genuine outpouring than this. And in some ways, the Emergent mess is like Jeroboam, who had come to reason with Rehoboam and was rejected, and proceeded to depart and start his own very un-anointed Kingdom.

Yes, we still have the shields. We still raise them as a show of power, prosperity and "purpose." But they are a cheap imitation of the Gold Shields of Glory God wanted for us. We have a FORM of godliness but deny the power thereof.

God is still looking for those who not settle for the bronze show, but who long for the REAL of God's Spirit. The word is always, "Return…remember…rebuild…" For God to raise up a true, anointed, Spirit-filled church, He needs those who recognize that what we have is

NOT the true. It is a substitute. He needs those who are willing to pay the price to halt the madness of doing just to do, building just to build, and working just to look busy and feel like we've got a purpose, who will abandon every human plan and seek the Lord for HIS way – HIS will - and HIS plan. He seeks those who will return to His will, remember how He works, and rebuild HIS house – one not of hands, but of heart, Spirit and truth. God give us that heart. May He return to us the Gold Shields that proclaim His glory and destroy from us the Brass shields that seek only to proclaim ours.

19 FINAL EXIT: HOW WILL THE CHURCH GO OUT?

"Nevertheless when the Son of man cometh, shall he find faith on the earth?" Luke 18:8b

Throughout scripture, God asks questions. In the beginning, he asked Adam, "Where are you? Who told you that you were naked?" And to Cain, "Where is your brother?" In this last hour, Jesus asks, "Will I find faith when I return?"

That answer, I believe, is quite up to us. I contend that we can go out with a roar, or with a whimper.

As I read and research volumes of spiritual information that comes to me regarding the "new wave" of spirituality which is manifesting in the world in such venues as "The Secret" and through such people as the High Priestess of the New Age, Oprah Winfrey, and is infecting the church through Purpose Driven, Emerging and the Post-Modern Church, I am overwhelmed by how quickly we are losing ground and how numb and naïve and fightless most believers are.

This morning I read and laid aside a long article filled with such torrents of information, and thought, "Well, then, how do we fight this? It appears the war is being won with nary a shot being fired from our side." Western Evangelical Christianity is bleeding to death, and the patient appears to just want more painkillers.

If I've learned anything the last few years, it is that most believers would rather not know all of this. I have lost both friends and supporters and gained opponents and mockers simply for saying, "Shouldn't we examine some of these new teachings before we support it or believe it?" Doing so has been a lot like telling your child there is no Santa. They will hate you for telling them before they accept that it is true. So much of the contemplative, emerging church dogma is filled with airy-fairy wishful thinking spirituality in which we heal the world and all you need is love, that when you point out that the whole of prophetic scripture opposes all of this dominionist "world future," you can almost see tears because you made a fairy die, and you can almost hear a call to all come together and hold hands and repeat, "I DO believe in fairies!" in order to silence the doubters and keep the "we are the world" fantasy alive. I don't mean to be overly sarcastic. I am just incredibly stunned and grieved that we no longer understand the nature of evil, the wickedness of the heart of unredeemed man, and the hopelessness of anything outside of the regenerative, powerful Gospel of Jesus Christ, a Gospel that does not say, "Heal the world" but instead urges us to pull people out of the fire because this present world order is "passing away" and WILL "melt away with a fervent heat." Where is that message?

I joke with my friends that I am the Grinch That Stole Everything, from Halloween to Henri Nouwen.

But none of it comes from the heart of a Grinch. It comes from a child of God who loves Jesus and loves His Word more than life. It comes from a heart, that upon recently learning that a well-meaning believer had led a group of kids through a "guided visualization meditation" to "Journey to Jesus," broke down and wept. "Jesus," I cried, "My life was nothing but occult lies when I came to You. It cost You – and me – EVERYTHING to get me free of those lies! WHY are believers believing and teaching and blindly accepting the SAME LIES that nearly destroyed me?"

So as I approach the latter half of my life, in what appears to be the latter part of man's history, I long to be one in whom Jesus WILL find faith when He comes. Not "I hope so" good thoughts or contemplative prayer out-of-body experiences, but real faith, RAW faith that plainly accepts every word of Jesus and lives like it, prays like it, preaches like it and acts on it.

God has always spoken of a remnant of His people. It is hard for us to accept that "broad is the way" that leads to destruction, and "narrow is the way" that leads to eternal life, and FEW are there that will find it. It is even more difficult to accept that there is also a "remnant" in the church. Most church folks are "A.M." Christians who like static and drifting stations and hopping from one channel to the next (every wind of doctrine) but there are also "F.M." believers who want to hear the truth clear and full of sound and soundness – steady, unchanging truth. There aren't a lot of F.M. Christians . Easier for most to "go along to get along" and not be bothered with the need to "contend for the faith" and to "perfect holiness in the fear of God."

It appears that the new spirituality is a huge package of sensual and experiential goodies that requires neither testing nor backbone to partake. Just…experience…it. (Are you "experienced"?) The face and words of Jesus are being redefined as we go along. It fits perfect in the New Age Era that is becoming like the Borg from Star Trek: "Resistance is futile. You will be assimilated. Your distinctiveness will be added to the Collective."

Not THIS little gray duck. A simple viewing of Disney's old nature film which shows hundreds of little rodent-like creatures called Lemmings following one Lemming off a cliff to their death is evidence that Majority Thinking, even in church, may not be healthy at all.

So what do we do? Give up? Wait for the world to end? Keep screaming the truth, even after the circus has put a sideshow sign on your calling?

If we know we are in the last times, then the warnings about the great falling away, mass spiritual deception and lying signs and wonders let us know where we are on the clock. In one sense, the time is coming when we can only "let the righteous be righteous still" and "let the filthy be filthy still". In other words, time is coming for a remnant to stand and let the Lemming believers run off the cliff if they insist on doing so. Oh, I know, that sounds arrogant; but what can you do when you realize that warnings and tears and Bible truth aren't even heard, when the Collective puts their fingers in their ears and says, "Nyah, Nyah, we can't HEEEARYOUUU!" Just let them go, I guess.

So what do we do then? I can't imagine it's God's will to crawl into a hole and wait for the end. And I don't believe that, either. The word has ALWAYS been to "occupy until I come." I believe, in fact, that this will be the real church's most glorious hour. For those who hold true to His Word, the waves of false teachings and occult spirituality and spineless, useless "Christianity" are in fact clarifying the truth and stripping away the dross, deception and darkness from true believers. It is removing the panicky sense of "The sky is falling! I must warn the King!" which has beset much of the last-days prophetic movement, and replacing it with, "I don't have to prove Jesus to anyone. I am not called to 'debate' or 'dialogue.'" Either Jesus is Lord or He is not. If people are determined to love the lie, let them. (They loved darkness rather than light, because their deeds were evil.) Just keep me in the truth, no matter the lies. And help me reach those who are in need of a real savior with real redeeming truth.

More now than ever, I see the line being drawn between those who want a religious experience, and those who want Jesus: those who want Romper Room, and those who want the Upper Room: those who seek knowledge and learning (Gnostic) and those who seek Truth that is embodied in the Word of God and in Jesus Himself: Those who crave powerful "events" and those who surrender to the Power of the Holy Spirit.

In the end, none of it will be about a war of words, or a way of worship, or a matter of opinion.

In the end, it will be, "Who is on the Lord's side?" It will not be about an ideology or theology – but a Person, Jesus Christ the Righteous Lord. And in the end, the difference between those who have given themselves over to lies and a "false Jesus" and those who have surrendered to the LORD Jesus and will be clear and devastating. The first will live in a world of false occult illusions disguised as "Christianity," and the other will walk in the true power of God. The first will have faith in trendy ideas and fantasies about a coming "extreme-earth-makeover" for God; the second will have faith only in a PERSON, Jesus Christ, knowing that they are just pilgrims on a search and rescue mission on a planet that is about to see its final days.

In the end, it will truly be the last Mount Carmel, the Elijahs who hold to truth and the Baal prophets who are covered with a thousand lies and demonic idols.

Both can pray. Both have ideas. Both even will have followings. (Although Elijah's wasn't but a handful.) But what mattered? "The God who answers by fire, HE is God." In the end, it's not who has the best ideas but who has the goods. Moses' staff will eat up Pharaoh's magicians' snakes. They may LOOK the same – but who will be endorsed and backed up by the power of the Living God? That is what counts.

But it won't be about raw power. I have always known that this last generation would be so filled with the love of God that it would overpower and overwhelm any darkness it touched. You see, this is the most fragmented and shattered generation in history. And sin unrestrained has caused, created and compounded it from generation to generation until we have a Frankenstein generation composed only of emotional and spiritual fragments. That's why the "emerging church" is like a spiritual cannibal that is taking pieces of other religions to cobble together a deformed version of "Christianity."

The New Age and all its spiritual counterfeits will push people to open their hearts to the "divine within" or the "universal mind" to get healed, providing a quick fix of "good feelings" while demonic forces numb them, control them, fragment them.

Into that darkness will come those who are filled with Jesus' love and with a healing fire in their hands and they will bring truth to shatter the lies, enraging the demons and demonized but bringing the Finger of God to those who cry out for Jesus, at once breaking their chains and healing them whole.

It will not be a word war in these closing hours, and it may be near time that those who see the truth will have to simply get out of the way of this cloud of deception that is upon the western church. Those who debate doctrinal nuances and dialogue with demons in the name of "understanding our common ground" may be left to dry up in the demonic dust of the coming storm of confusion.

But out of that dust storm will come an army of shining sons and daughters who will blaze through the night with the preaching of Peter, the wisdom and warrior skills of Deborah, the intercessory guts of Esther, the power of Paul, the compassion of John, the boldness of Elijah, the anointing of Moses and the heart of David.

We can be part of that company, and be written in the annals of eternity and be counted among those who stayed faithful and true to the end, cost what it may…

…or be among those who whimpered their way to the end, covered in compromise, weakness and spineless religion…buried and forgotten in the dust of this last war.

What a sobering – and eternally vital – choice we must all make. May God give you – and I – the fortitude to make the only one that matters for eternity. When the Son of Man comes, may He find strong, vital and life-changing faith – in us.

20 NEUTRALIZATION OF THE CHURCH IN PREPARATION FOR THE COMING ANTICHRIST

(Note: Some of these warnings were first written in an article I wrote called "The Trojan Horse.") This article is an updated understanding based on the current conditions within the evangelical church in the Western world – G.R.)

Jesus said the gates of hell would not prevail against the church. The church is those who gather together in His Name to do His Will and spread His Gospel. And truly, that church will not fail. But then, that must mean that most of what we see in Evangelical, post-modern, emerging religious circles is not "the church" but rather a form of religion that has the word trappings of the church but has not the power, nor the mandate, nor the authority that comes only from the Word of God and the power of the Holy Spirit. It is just a physical shell made up of lost people who for some reason have been drawn to a religious place and religious ideas but have not been drawn into total abandonment to Jesus and surrendered to His absolute Lordship. They are those Paul speaks of who have "a form of godliness but deny the power thereof." (2 Timothy 3:5) This is why Paul told us to "examine yourselves, whether you be in the faith"(2 Cor.13:5), because obviously, even back then you could be in the CHURCH without being in the FAITH. He then gave the criteria: Jesus Christ is IN you, unless you are reprobate. In other words, if Jesus does not live IN you, you are not His. Your life must belong to Jesus, lock stock and barrel.

"Accepting" Jesus is a modern invention. As Keith Green used to point out, Jesus doesn't have a self-image problem where He needs our "acceptance." We need Him to accept US, and He will only do that when we come to the cross and surrender our old lives. I fear that most of the modern church is a group of nice people who are attracted to the nice ideas of Jesus and family and church but have never been to the altar and cried out for His mercy and forgiveness for their sins and surrendered their lives over to His Lordship. And that, friends, is what being a "Christian" is.

The modern church mix is made up of many people of the first order, who are drawn to the ideas and trappings of church but who are not the surrendered property of Jesus, and those of the second, those who HAVE surrendered to Jesus at some point, but who have grown weary in well-doing and have laid down their mantles as watchmen and simply allowed all the new changes in "church" to come in without examining it, and without contesting the wrong in it, and without taking a stand against the increasing infiltration of occult new age lies, because they are…worn out. And the third group is a small group who know what is coming and who are being marginalized because they raise the warning cry.

In order for the one world order/ one world religion to succeed and make the way for the antichrist to come to power, the first group has to be recognized as the "church," the second group of real believers needs to be neutralized, put to sleep or worn out to be too weak to fight, and the third must be marginalized, criticized, mocked and dismissed so they will no longer be part of the emerging "Church" but will be considered outcasts, extremists and freaks.

This is how it will be accomplished:

1. They will change the vocabulary of the church.

Much like a spiritual Orwellian nightmare, the "antiquated and alienating" language of the church will be replaced with a whole new dictionary of catch-phrase, cute and pithy rhyming bromides, tips and spiritual soundbites, as well as new-age friendly and interchangeable words and phrases. Not acceptable will be the words sin, repentance, the coming of Jesus, tribulation, heaven, eternal life, judgment, the cross, the blood of Jesus, suffering, chastisement, Lord Jesus. Instead, the new dictionary is going to be a mass of herd-thinking, Lemming-following modern words and phrases designed to brainwash and get us all "on the same page" (to use one newspeak phrase) and includes these weak and powerless substitutions for "that old time religion" talk: Paradigm shift, emergent, enlightenment, transformation, seeker-friendly, dialoguing, sacred tribes, (instead of cults and witches and pagans and Satanists) Jesus as Leader and Director (not Lord), Kingdom Now, Kingdom Come, As Above So Below, world changers, dream seekers, vision casting, changing direction or changing our way of thinking (instead of repenting), centering, contemplative prayer, dream catchers, reformation, etc.

Once all the words that have always defined and established the Gospel as not just words but power are eliminated, then this new vocabulary will become like an exclusive language that will make the "old talkers" look like outdated, "unenlightened" and non-progressive spiritual has-beens and relics from a less "transformed" time.

Since the New Age dictionary is the template for all the new emergent "churchspeak," all the new "emergents" will indeed be on "the same page" – right out of Satan's playbook for absorbing and neutralizing the "church". It will make that church as powerless as a toothless poodle.

2. They will gut the power of the Word of God.

This is being done through several very deliberate means. First, they are glutting the Christian marketplace with new translations, most of them based on a spurious text that was disregarded as flawed for centuries, then reworked by two British occultists (Westcott & Hort – check your translation and you may see their names in there) and has been the text that has been pushed as the text on which almost ALL new Bible versions are based, from NIV to New Century. Then they throw in a glut of Bible "paraphrases," which are not translations but just a person's idea of what they think it means, such as The Message. As the one reliable (KJV) translation becomes a relic that is unwelcome in the Emergent Church, Satan delights on seeing the look of confusion on people's faces as one verse goes up on Power Point and ten different people have ten different translations that aren't even close to what is on the screen – and they quietly conclude, "This is confusing. I'll just stop reading it for myself. " This is why so few kids ever show up in church with a Bible and just trust that whatever goes up on the screen is okay.

Being that hundreds of references to Jesus' Lordship, the Cross, sin and the Blood of Jesus are routinely (and often randomly, based on the translator's bias) removed, soon the power and authority of God's Word will be taken out of the church and left with the few who dare to actually believe it IS God's perfect Word. This new "church" and new "youth paradigm" will be one that uses scripture only as a "helpful guide." Kids will no longer be encouraged to "study to show yourself approved unto God" but instead will be fed "experience" as more important than the Bible. The power – and the importance – of preaching and teaching will be downplayed and even mocked. This quest for "experience" will be a gateway to massive deception, as one experience opens up to another. Those who challenge the experiences if they do not line up with scripture will be called Bible thumpers, extremists, Pharisees, and those who are limiting the Holy Spirit.

As parents and church leaders stop putting a premium on the Word of God, then kids will simply not take it seriously anymore. An encouragement to "quiet time" will become little more than a scripture bite with "contemplative" activities, "breath prayers," and other Hindu-drawn devices. The scriptures will become meaningless, or, at most, a nice guide to better living.

How far this is from the sacred Word of God that has cost MILLIONS of believers their LIVES just to possess even a PORTION of it over the centuries!

After enough new Bible versions have filled the church so that while we're all "on the same page" NO ONE will on the same page, because the pages and words are so different, and when enough "inclusive" language is put in the new Bibles to replace the old, there will come a "new age" version that even Hindus, Buddhists Wiccans and Pagans can accept. And I believe it is already being worked on as I write. By the time it is brought out and hailed as the inclusive, definitive Bible for all ages, those who contend for the purity and authority of the Word of God will be so mocked and dismissed that they will be, to these "new age believers," nothing more than a joke and an annoyance.

3. They must bring the church into paganization through syncretism.

This is a program-in-progress even now, where, degree by degree, we "lower the bar" of truth in order to let unchurched people gain entrance – not to the Kingdom of God – but to this new church.

In this church, there will be no speaking of the occult or occult practices as "bad", no talk of other religions as bad, no speaking of Jesus as the only way. It will be the church that only accentuates the positive and eliminates the negative (positive and negative are also big newspeak words in this church), and it will grow exponentially as witches, occultists, homosexuals, radical feminists, socialists, adulterers and pedophiles realize this is a church that asks no questions, raises no standard and requires no repentance. "Come as you are" the new banner, will never add, "Go and sin no more." There will be no uncomfortability, no challenge, no conviction. This church will be big on works and become the perfect "model" for the one world order who will compel people to "heal the world" rather than prepare for His return. It will be a socialist club that will kiss the face of the Buddhist priest as they fall into eternal hell, join hands with the gay pastor in the pulpit who will go and engage those same hands in detestable and forbidden perversions and they will call him "godly" and thus fill up the blasphemy of the Whore of Babylon and re-establish the Baal prophets and homosexual prostitutes in the very house of God.

As the church is being moved away from expecting a "pie in the sky by and by", and moved toward a socialistic works oriented religion that will take the place of social programs, it will be moving exactly into the place it was designed to by those who control the Luciferian agenda and do not want to eliminate the evangelical church, but neutralize, co-opt and absorb it. For this Luciferian order does not wish to destroy the world, but to make it a PERFECT world – disease free, poverty free, war-free – only with Lucifer as god and not Jesus as Lord of all. The move for the emergent church to be pushed toward "repairing the world" and be overwhelmingly involved in social and political causes is all part of the plan.

4. Lying Signs and Wonders Are Coming.

As the wall of truth is torn down and a "new wall of understanding and interpreting truth" is put up with untempered mortar, I see a huge crack or gap in the back wall of the church. In the midst of this church will be souls hurting and hungry for the supernatural power of God. (As we should be hungry.) But there will be a multitude who are NOT exercised in the Word of God to discern truth from lie. They have not been taught, nor do they practice, how to "try the spirits, to see whether they be of God". They will seek an EXPERIENCE with God (as we should!) but the boundary of truth cannot protect them, and has not been established IN them through years of commitment to the engrafted and written Word.

This will provide a spiritual crack that is going to allow a trickle, then a stream, then a flood of supernatural events to fill this new church. I am grieved and hesitant to say, that I believe much of this is going to come through the new "prophetic" movement.

Now, hear me – I was spiritually raised Pentecostal, I believe in all the gifts and manifestations of the Holy Spirit, and I believe we need them now more than any time in history. I am both an intercessor and a watchman. I believe, I believe I BELIEVE! – in ALL of God's Holy Spirit miracle power! And I LONG for it!

But I am also a former occultist, and I have fought those powers all of my life. And I tell you before God, that Satan can imitate it ALL. I have heard tongues and prophecy and heard Gospel hymns and choruses in a spiritualist church. I have seen demonic healings and lying signs and wonders that would make the hair on the back of your neck stand up.

And I tell you, as much as I see the need for the prophetic and believe much of it is from God, I am seeing that a great deal of it is NOT. It is guessing, speculation, elaborate wordworking, and UNTESTED. The scriptures could not be more plain to "believe not every spirit." I am concerned because a generation raised and conditioned and bathed in the occult through media and books, CAN NOT NATURALLY DISCERN an occult working from the Holy Spirit! And the door has opened to "satisfy" the "seekers of the supernatural" who do not, because they have not been trained how to, "test the spirits." They are not being told to test the spirits, lest they be "doubting God" and "limiting the Spirit." This breach in truth will give way to "lying signs and wonders", "sanctified" necromancy (that is already happening), meaningless miracles (what purpose does gold dust serve?) and direct "prophecy" from lying spirits. A church "open to anything" is going to fall prey to EVERYTHING.

This particular phase is crucial to those who are "preparing the way" for "the one" as they call him whose coming is with all lying signs and wonders. The "new church" will only see the power he shows and count it as being from God.

Folks, I believe in the real power and miracle supernatural of God more now than I ever have. For that reason I raise this warning. ALL THAT GLITTERS IS NOT GOD! Test it ALL!

1. The final step: Eliminate the Apocalyptic.

NONE of the new age agenda or one world – one religion can succeed unless the biggest obstacle is removed from the evangelical church as it stands: The preaching of the return of Jesus Christ in the clouds, the coming tribulation and the end of all things.

Tribulation, persecution, revelation, the second coming, the rapture, ALL that must be eliminated from vocabulary and preaching and teaching in the "emerging church" if they are to succeed in co-opting the evangelical church. And we're almost there NOW. Just this morning, I read these frightening words from a "prophetic" conference: "We must stop erroneous thinking to escape with the rapture. Let's repent of this! Church mentality is RENTING. But God is into owning the whole thing!" (Earth.)

Here we see the crux of this new thinking: "Kingdom Now." "The Kingdom is WITHIN and AMONG you!" "Thy Will be done on earth…NOW."

Many scriptures are being twisted and de-contextualized to condition the church, not to expect Jesus' return (at least not from heaven and in the clouds), not to prepare their lamps with oil, but to TAKE OVER. It's called "dominion theology." And it is going to send a whole multitude of naïve and non-discerning believers into a trap of thinking they are going to rule on earth but will instead face a prison and persecution of believers such as the world has never seen. I didn't say it; Jesus did. Read Matthew 24.

A thorough and honest reading of the New Testament makes it abundantly clear that Jesus will return in the clouds, and that the church is to EXPECT Him – to literally "love His appearing." The words of prophecy concerning the last days are abundant and numerous.

So why is it that this generation is completely unfamiliar with all of this? When it the last time you heard a message on Jesus' return, or last days events, or preparation?
I fear, for whatever good the "Left Behind" book series did, the damage may be greater, because now, well, it's all…fiction. Fiction stories.

In order for the coming antichrist agenda to succeed, he must have a church that says, "Where is the promise of his coming? For since the fathers fell asleep, all things continue as they were from the beginning of the creation." (2 Peter 3:4) Are we not almost there now? Have not those who preach Jesus' soon return, who warn of coming tribulation and judgment, been categorized and dismissed as "doomsday preachers", people to be laughed at and mocked, or at least, have people roll their eyes at them in mild amusement and pity?

Watch for the "emerging church" to rapidly redefine and explain away and change the meaning of all the scriptures that deal with prophecy and the last days. And since most new "church" folks don't read the Bible for themselves, the issue will rarely even come up.

Rather than pilgrims and strangers whose home is in heaven, who believe to "be with Christ, which is far better", who know the kingdom is invisible and who know we are not here to" heal the world" but to "call every man to repentance", this new church will become little more than the relief social agency for this coming world system of antichrist, and whose inclusion in that system will give them a false religious sense of "purpose" and "destiny" and "doing good works", as they lose the true mandate: to preach the fiery gospel of Jesus because they know that "the end of all things is at hand."

It is difficult to believe, but the day will come when who Jesus was and is will be so redefined and changed, and what He said about His coming will be so twisted, that the "man of peace" may come, and many of these new "emergent" church believers will say, "We got it wrong! He HAS come back, just not as we thought! He's come back as a human, and he's got the love, and the miracles, and the power to prove it!" And thus the deception – and the way – for the end of things – will be complete and ready to begin the final countdown.

I cannot bring myself to end this on a positive note, lest I detract from the gravity of what I have written and been shown. I will only say, to those who have ears to hear, hold your ground; be strong; behave like men and women of the living God; put on all your armor, watch, and earnestly contend for the faith that was delivered to you; keep your bags packed and hold everything lightly in your hands; preach the uncompromised word that makes people sweat, get angry, and walk away or repent and weep and get saved; do not compromise; prepare for hard times; and look up and REJOICE, because your redemption is drawing nigh!

Man the outposts! Hold the line. Be the warrior. Do not back down. Stand firm in the truth, and the gates of hell WILL NOT PREVAIL against those who stand and fight to the last!

21 LIFE & DEATH

I have a deep concern for this new generation of church folks and church kids. Perhaps it has been a concern for a long time, but I am beginning to see it with a new clarity.

One of the major downfalls of the "seeker friendly" churches is that we can rarely be sure why people are there. Is it genuine spiritual seeking – or is it because it's friendly, fun and family-oriented? (The Mormons have that.) I'm realizing more and more how easy it is for people to get into the "God thing." Especially since, well, it's safe, moral, and harmless. Better than raising kids without those things, right?

Unfortunately, we are in danger of losing the one dynamic that makes the Kingdom of God real, and different from all other religions – RESURRECTION LIFE.

I've been concerned for some time because this generation of Christian kids, for the most part, doesn't even know how to lead someone to Jesus. Lately I've been concerned because many of them are not even very clear on what a Christian IS. They know it has to do with church, taking communion, prayer, being moral, and believing in Jesus. My concern is you can have all of that…and still not be saved.

You can believe in Jesus and still not be saved? Sure. James said, "You believe that there is one God. You do well. Even the demons believe – and tremble! (James 2:19) I believe in the President. I believe in many of his ideas, even. But I do not KNOW him. I just know ABOUT Him. In the same way, many know about Jesus but do not have a personal relationship with him. There is a big difference.

The phrase "born again Christian" was the right concept, but soon became a semi-derogatory term. Now it's rarely used to define what a Christian is.

Jesus said, "Assuredly I tell you, unless one is born again, he cannot see the kingdom of God." (John 3:3) First birth – natural. Second birth – spiritual, eternal. It is not a set of ideas but a transformation, from the kingdom of darkness to the kingdom of His Son, from death to life.

We have largely exchanged the truth of the resurrection life for a kind of spiritual home improvement. Jesus makes you better, nicer, happier. But we leave out the cross.

And here is where we have missed the mark. Recently I read a quote that hit me so hard that it plunged a sword straight into my heart. I want you to prepare your own heart to receive this truth, because it is absolutely crucial that we understand it and apply it:

Jesus doesn't take bad people and make them good. He takes dead people and makes them alive.

Until we nail down this essential truth of the Gospel, we cannot fully understand – nor convey – the true meaning of "Christian."

Being a Christian, then, is not about how you live, or what you believe (although both of these things are VITAL if you are a Christian) but it is about WHO YOU BELONG TO. A Christian is one who has consciously handed over complete ownership of their life to Jesus. It is someone who has come to the cross, and seen with perfect clarity their sinfulness, their deadness, and cried for Him to exchange their sin and death for His life. There is no other way.

"If anyone is in Christ, he is a new creation." (2 Cor. 5:17) A new species. Not a dressed-up, heavily make-upped version of the old one. That's what a funeral home does: they try to make the dead look good one last time. Too often that is what we do. We put the makeup of Christian trappings on church folks, hoping the clothes will somehow transform them. No! It does not work that way.

This problem has become clear to me in my attempting to help kids know how to find the "right one." I'm pretty clear about this up-front. Do not date an unbeliever. Period! "Do not be unequally yoked together with unbelievers." (1 Cor. 6:14a) Paul's words were based on a clear understanding that we were of a different species.

I don't know how many people I've known that ignored this verse, to the thwarting of God's plan for them. They married an unbeliever, believing they would get saved. 40 years later, nothing. Some kids date unbelievers thinking they can save them. Rarely happens. And the trap is, once they begin to bond with an unbeliever, the delusion grows. They think if they share their faith, it will "draw a line" and the other person will say, "Oh heck no, I'm not dating a Christian." Instead, if they are already attracted, the other person will play the game of, "Well, what kind of a Christian do you want me to be? I can be that." They'll learn the church thing and the God talk and play the Jesus card and all the rest – just to marry the person (or worse, as often happens, just get them into bed.) Only later does the naïve believer learn that it was just an act.

"But they are a good person, moral, even believe in God. Isn't that better than dating a drinker, druggie, or someone who sleeps around?" The answer is, it doesn't matter how "moral" they are – why are you dating a corpse? Satan loves nothing more than to trap Christian kids into believing their faith will "rub off" somehow and the corpse will become alive. No! That ONLY happens through transformational encounter with the Living God in Jesus Christ. NO OTHER WAY! And I always tell kids, unless you are 100% per cent sure the person you are interested in loves Jesus as much or more than you – and aren't afraid to tell people that – don't get anywhere near them.

I once heard someone got engaged, and their fiancée said, "I will NEVER love you more than Jesus. If you're going to try to change that, we're not getting married."

You should not settle for anything but that kind of commitment in a potential mate. God's not into "fixer-uppers."

When you begin to truly understand the difference between being born again and being spiritually dead, then your mission to the world changes. You're not here to offer marriage tips, cool "Christian" music or nice invites to potlucks. You are one a life and death rescue mission. Those around you who do not belong to Jesus are dead, and you cannot fix them. We need to stop trying to make the church attractive to unbelievers. Where in the world did we get that ungodly, unscriptural concept? The church is not there to attract the dead but to RAISE THE DEAD TO LIFE!

Our message inside and outside the church should never be, "Try Jesus, you'll like Him" but rather, "Jesus ALONE can save you from eternal death." It stops being an accommodating lure message and becomes a challenge to darkness and evil to give up their dead.

Open our eyes, precious Jesus, to see that we are not an entertainment center with a positive message, or a cultural center where we can learn to get along. Help us to see that the church is an E.R., and we, each of us, are its medics. End the confusion brought on by so many years of weak preaching that we cannot even define what a true believer is anymore. Help us to understand that we are resurrected light-bearers, truth-tellers and life-givers in Jesus, and that only when we truly see the unredeemable death in those around us – no matter how moral or religious - can we shine the light of Jesus and say, "Lazarus, COME FORTH!"

22 REMOVING THE LINCHPIN

Satan fears the Word of God. I've lived enough to see the power of the Word of God change lives, heal the sick, deliver from demons, mend broken hearts, and set people on fire with purpose and power.

I was recently "set" up in a phone interview I did innocently believing I was going to be asked about my law enforcement work. Instead, I was viciously attacked. At one point, they said, "You're not law enforcement. You have no formal training. What right do you have to post what you do on the internet?" "Because it's the truth", I replied. "That's YOUR truth!" they replied. I nearly laughed. I'd hit the crux of the matter. "Listen bubba", I replied, "There's no 'my truth' and 'your truth'. A thing is either true or it's not."

If I said I was a poached egg, you would call a therapist. "But that's MY truth!" No, that's my DELUSION. Clearly I am not a poached egg (though I sometimes resemble one.)

Somehow, absolute truth has been completely lost in the modern lie of "relativism" – you know – that truth is subject to circumstances, social settings and personal feelings. One professor told a student, "There are no absolutes", to which the wise student replied, "Are you absolutely sure?"

The degree in which relativism has infested the educational system and filled young minds full of junk is deeply disturbing. I can't even have a rational conversation with most "educated" people. They get emotional and angry when presented with reason and facts that contradict their oft-repeated and little reasoned ten second sound bite opinions, finally ending the conversation with, "Well, that's YOUR truth!" Which is the liberal version of "Nanny, nanny boo boo!"

Can you imagine, if, for example, driving laws were based on relativism?

- The lights are red, yellow, and green. If your truth says red means go, then go.
- The speed limit is only a suggested one. If it "feels right" to go 90 MPH in a school zone, follow your heart.

In other words, lawlessness and anarchy would rule the road, and it would be a slaughter, when "your truth" opposed "mine" and we met in a fatal crash of relativistic speed limit interpretations.

Can you imagine if scientists worked by that standard? We'd never have gotten to the moon. "it's about a million miles…we think…but we only use the rule as a 'general guideline'. The moon looks closer by eye, so we trust that more than some 'absolute ruler.'"

Obviously we don't conduct science OR road laws by relativism.

But we ARE told by the world to conduct our lives that way. Paul calls it "the Spirit of lawlessness." It is the ageless satanic lie that says that you can become your own god.

Now that most of the world is under the influence of this lie, Satan has now set his sites on the church. The church has always been most powerful when it has proclaimed the pure Word of God. Satan knows it is his biggest threat.

For hundreds of years, he's been successful at weakening the church through petty doctrinal differences: methods of baptism, tongues, end-time disputes.

Now, he's about to go for the jugular. He is seeking to completely destroy the standard of truth – the Word of God – in the house of God.

The Bible is the standard – the linchpin, so to speak – the foundation of truth by which we live. All else – relationships, righteousness, directions and destiny – hinge on it, our ability to stay true to it. God Himself set that linchpin – "Forever, O Lord, Your Word is settled in heaven." (Ps. 119:89) "Heaven and earth will pass away, but My words will never pass away." (Mt.24:35) And woe be to those who tamper with it!

But tampering they are, to their own destruction.

Two young people I love dearly attended the same Christian Bible school, where they were subjected to a book that contained a chapter that convincingly argued that the Bible really did NOT condemn homosexuality. Talk about confusing! You go to a Bible School to learn about the Bible, and they undermine the very thing they claim to stand for!

We used to joke about seminaries, calling them "cemeteries" and now I don't think we were too far off the mark. I will be accused of being anti-intellectual, which is fine. I've got to tell you, I've rarely seen someone argued into the Kingdom of God. Even the great CS Lewis came to Jesus by a burst of spontaneous revelation riding his bike, not by argument. People come into the Kingdom, not by good ideas, but because God opens their hearts to truth. And yes, there is a place for reasoned argument, as Paul speaks to persuading people. But it always strikes me that although Festus said, "Paul, you almost persuade me to become a Christian", we don't know that he ever did.

But my concern isn't just that we're too intellectual. In fact, there are too many believers that "only believe" but haven't a CLUE as to why! I always encourage kids to learn all they can, get all the facts and think sharp so they can "be ready to give an answer to every man for the hope that is within you." (1 Pet. 3:15) Nevertheless, the rise of Christian intellectual elitism that is pervading many seminaries, Christian media and churches is a concern. I realize I am not a scholar. I can't argue didactic points (or even tell you what didactic means) or give grand outlines. I'm just a truth-teller. And I expect the world to react negatively to what I say and write. But 90% of the assault I get comes from Christians who think I'm too subjective, too "experiential." Or, too fundamental". I get it from both ends. I stand in the middle and believe that experiencing God is totally compatible with 100% faith in the Scriptures. In fact it is only when these things become one dynamic that the Kingdom is truly manifest in power.

But given the option of being too "fundamental" or too "experiential", based on the dangerous place I see a lot of Christians, I'll take "fundamental."

For many, that reads as "Pharisee." But the Pharisee's problem wasn't that they believed the Scriptures; it's that (a) they added a thousand laws and inferences not there, and (b) They did not grasp the TRUTH of the scriptures; "You search the scriptures, thinking you will find eternal life; but these are they that speak of Me." (John 5:39)

In other words, they took the Word and tried to make it say what they WANTED it to say. You can't do that.

I recently had a conversation concerning "Do not be unequally yoked with unbelievers." (2 Cor. 6:14) Someone had told a young person I know that it was referring to business deals, not marriage. (The logic of that, of course, is absurd – implying that God cares more about keeping our business dealings separate from unbelievers, but in the most spiritual human relationship of all – marriage – it doesn't matter!) I sat in shock, as this young person said this man had been living with an unbeliever, and she later got saved. (Maybe she did. I pray so and rejoice if so.) The young man I spoke to asked if this guy was in trouble; after all, he was doing well, and was financially blessed, his wife got saved – didn't that indicate God's blessing?

First, I explained, his finances were irrelevant. Second, I said, he's in more trouble than he knows. HE BELIEVES A LIE. Rather than take God's Word at face value concerning not being unequally yoked, he said, "It doesn't fit how I'm living. I've got to see it in a way so I can make it fit my lifestyle." Peter spoke of those who "twist the scriptures, to their own destruction." (2 Pet.3:16)

Worse – he was teaching kids the same thing! I would rather be living in abject sinful failure and proclaim, "I may be in sin, but the Word of God is still true", than to gloss over the scriptures to cover up my violation of it. It's about integrity to TRUTH.

Anytime we run into scriptures that speak in opposition to cultural sins or our personal ones – we choose to either receive the truth regardless, or we end up twisting what is there to make it support sin.

Never – NEVER – bend the Word of God to fit around your sins or lifestyle. Bend – and break – your own hardened sinful heart and conform to its truth. Fall on the rock and be broken, Jesus said, or it will fall on you and crush you to powder. (Mt. 21:44) "Is not my Word like a rock…like a hammer?" (Jer. 23:29)

If my EXPERIENCE contradicts the scriptures – my experience is wrong. Period. If my way of life contradicts it – my way of life must change. It's that simple.

I recently read an article by a mother about keeping kids away from the occult. She agreed with all the scriptures against it. Then she explained how they read Harry Potter with their kids, explaining the GOOD, pointing out the bad. (Either make the tree good and its fruit good, Jesus said, or make the tree bad and its fruit bad – Matthew 12:33) She did the usual delusional justification of the difference between "real" magic and "fantasy magic."

Then, in a stunning piece of advice, she tells parents to steer children away from things that were about talking to the dead, divination or spell-casting!

She apparently was completely blind to the fact that Potter was FILLED with spell-casting, teachers who were divinators and the DEAD speaking through the living!

This is a perfect example of moving the linchpin even a little. She moved it just a hair – "Well, the scriptures are probably only condemning REAL magic, not fantasy magic…" The next thing you know, she's so deceived, in one breath she can tell you to avoid occult practices, and in the next, promotes a story FULL of them – without a CLUE to the contradiction! Once you move the linchpin just a little, it's just the beginning.

Someone told me, "I don't accept a certain part of the Bible." I said, "Well, then throw the whole thing in the trash and get it over with. Because if you can't trust THAT part, why trust ANY of it? How do you know ANY of it is trustworthy if you just throw out what you don't like?"

NO. Accept it ALL or accept NONE.

That doesn't mean it's all easy to understand. Far from it. Many times I feel like I did when I was a child, crying, yelling, staring at math problems and saying, "I DON'T GET IT!!!" How foolish to abandon math, because it does not always make sense to ME, therefore it must not be true. It's my understanding that is lacking, not the material.

I play a frustrating computer game where you have to combine similar objects to get points. As the clock runs down, I can rarely find the combinations to keep the game running. But it's THERE. On occasion, I just take a deep breath, relax, and tell myself, "You can find it. It's right there somewhere." And there it is. The game didn't lie; I just couldn't see what was there.

I've always approached the Word of God that way. If I'm confused or don't get something, I say, "The answer is here. Show me, Father." And He does. Sometimes the answer was right in front of me, not able to see it without the Holy Spirit's help.

Math does not lie. It's fundamental truth. The Word of God does not lie; it is fundamental truth. Change one math fundamental, you produce chaos. Change one little iota of scripture, then spiritual chaos will follow.

In a time when churches and even denominations are trying to remove the linchpin of the Scriptures to justify adultery, homosexuality, occultism, you name it, in a time when "new translations" are hip and seeker-friendly and the "Old" are being buried by them, it is imperative that men and women of God who guard that linchpin nail it in solid, guard it and TEACH it to this generation, who will be the guardians of the Word of God for the generation to come.

As an old preacher once said, "God said it. I believe it. That settles it." It's just like that. Anything less is tampering with the Word of God, to our own destruction.

23 THE GATHERING STORM

Many of life's difficult and painful things are not sudden, but slow events: bankruptcy, divorce, terminal illness.

But we are not shielded from the many devastating sudden tragedies, either. We are geared to "eat, drink and be merry." When sudden tragedy hits, we are…unprepared. Jesus said, "…until the flood came and took them all away." Because they ignored Noah, the eccentric, annoying, divisive boat-builder, they were swept away in a second.

Jesus wept a heartbreaking warning over Jerusalem. They ignored him and in 72 A.D., it all came to an end for them.

Elijah warned, "Choose". Then the fire came.

Lot was warned, and escaped. His wife looked back and died.

It is not an accident that the last book of the Bible is the Revelation of Jesus, a book packed with dire warnings, cataclysm and prophetic endings. No wonder it's the least-preached book!

It's amazing how much of the New Testament letters are words of warning and preparation. "Wake up! Don't be deceived. Be sober. Expect hard times. Be ready!" Not much about how to succeed, get wealthy or lose weight. The New Testament books are preparatory warfare books. If they needed them then, how much more now that we see the end of all things approaching?

But there is so little of that anymore. I had a dream yesterday. There was once a man not long ago with a powerful prophetic voice – Keith Green. He was unashamed to weep, to preach truth no matter what the cost. He died in early 1981, and in my view, no musical voice has come to fill the void.

In my dream, he was on stage, and I was in the church crowd. He looked out – and wept. I was suddenly hit with a conviction – a grief – that was so strong that I hung my head in shame and wept. I woke up sobbing.

Where have our tears gone? We do not weep for the lost. We do not weep for the broken, the rejected, we do not weep tears of sorrow over our own spiritual lukewarmness.

Even though the church is becoming infected with sin and compromise on every side, we do not see it, because we are content and we do not want to be disturbed. The dream I had reminded me of one of Keith's lyrics:

The world is sleeping in the dark
But the church just can't fight
Because it's asleep in the light,
How can you be so dead
When you've been so well-fed?

I truly believe Satan's greatest accomplishment is not making believers sin but in making them NUMB. "Woe to those who are at ease in Zion."

My tears come because I hunger for a fiery word – of conviction, of revelation, of truth – truth that COULD make me weep, and cry to God for more, for full surrender of my complacent life.

My call to ministry came in 1973 when I received a recorded message from David Wilkerson called, "The Vision." I listened with fear and awe as he related how God kept him up several nights revealing what was coming to the world and the church.

Among other things, God showed him the Soviet Union would collapse. That was ABSURD in 1973- Now, the young grow up in a world without it. Mocked, reviled, David's vision has nearly all been fulfilled, including God showing him a demonic "baptism of filth" was coming on the earth (this was before the internet) and a "persecution madness" that was going to come against believers here in the states.

My reaction to that message was to fall on my knees in holy fear and cry out, "God, make me ready! I surrender ALL to Your service!" Within 3 months I was in Bible School preparing. The rest, you know.

Over the years, every single moment of radical change in my life has come just as "The Vision" did – through a fiery, heaven-breathed Word. I rarely hear such words anywhere, though somewhere ,they must be being preached.

Instead, the only time I see believers emotionally stirred seems to be through almost nursery-rhyme little stories designed to tug the heartstrings toward God, Mr. Rogers-like stories. We tell kids fluffy stories and end up with fluffy, spiritually weak kids.

That is NOT the Word that overwhelms us and changes us radically. We are nearly dead we are so numb and we do not need feel-good-about-God fixes, but jarring, transforming TRUTH.

As I have said before, the storm is on the horizon. The riptide of secular antichrist hatred for everything righteous or Biblical which reached a near boil last year has receded - to plan, To organize. And to begin to time the triggers they have already placed within the educational system, the courts, the media and the special interest groups such as the ACLU, the NEA and the Gay Alliances – and within a generation of non-thinking children and youth – timed to go off and retake lost territory and silence once for all the mouth of believers who dare to believe in Biblical truth. By and large, our children are not prepared for the onslaught they will face. My obsessive drive to teach Kids the Word of God is driven by this understanding of the coming storm.

How do we prepare for this coming storm?

1. Teach the Whole Truth. It is time to consider stopping giving people – and ourselves – "bite-size snack" messages and begin real, comprehensive, equipping lessons that will provide believers with real tools to combat the lies.

2. Teach our kids to STAND. Most kids are too timid or intimidated to challenge the growing antichristian, anti-Bible ridicule and politically bent attacks by students, teachers and professors that pass as "education." (No wonder 87% of Christian kids lose their faith after entering college!)

When we were in High School, we were on fire for Jesus, and we did not know that we should not talk. You could not have stopped us! A Methodist minister who taught Comparative Religion was teaching that the Bible was a myth and that Jesus was just a good man, not the Son of God. Respectfully but firmly, a Christian friend and I raised our hands and challenged him. We made his class MISERABLE for him. While today, we'd be afraid of being considered "disruptive", then we were simple exercising our free speech rights and making sure HE didn't use the class to brainwash and hoist his antichrist opinion on students instead of doing what he was paid to – TEACH OBJECTIVELY. Our kids should be so equipped; and if they get ridiculed, harassed and get into trouble, good for them. Let's support them. There's plenty of Christian legal centers that can help kids challenge the kind of antichrist attacks that are so prevalent – and growing – on campuses against Christian kids.

3. Teach our youth Biblical truth on relevant issues that they WILL be challenged on: Evolution, the occult, abortion, homosexuality, premarital sex, etc. We're too focused on "how to date," "self-image," etc., keeping our kids INWARD and self-focused. We have GOT to break the siege mentality – the "let's just stay very still and hope no one notices us" fear-based way of conducting ourselves in this world. Having kids Biblically equipped on specific things will be a necessity if we want them to survive and THRIVE. Even now, some middle schools have "diversity and tolerance" weeks where kids have to sign a pledge to support and ACCEPT the gay way of life! One has to ask what in the WORLD that has to do with education. It is in fact SOCIAL ENGINEERING and kids are a SOCIAL EXPERIMENT for the National Education Association and others. And the fact is, a number of kids won't even TELL their parents about such a pledge. Often they are encouraged NOT to. (Kids love secrets.)

We need to avail ourselves of the excellent resources such as Dr. Kent Hoeven's Creation series (www.drdino.com), Exodus International's Biblical and restoration ministry for those seeking out of homosexuality and equipping believers to be informed and ready to teach the truth on this volatile issue (www.exodusinternational.org). David Limbaugh has written an excellent, chilling and in my view MANDATORY book called "Persecution" which documents the social agenda to silence believers and what to do about it. If we are willing to invest in vital instructional tools for our kids, they are out there.

4. Get educated and prepared.

I'm alarmed by what kids are telling me goes on in schools. Same-sex couples making out in hallways. Teachers who share "drinking recipes" with their students, teachers who flirt with students, as well as students who are carrying on clandestine affairs with their teachers, teachers who are introducing all manner of occult and sexual garbage into the class that has NOTHING to do with the class curriculum. There has never been a more crucial time for parents to be hands-on. Talk to your kids about every class, every subject and every teacher. Find out what kinds of plays are done, what kinds of in-school activities and clubs and workshops are being carried out. It is a MISTAKE to believe the educational system has your child's –

or your – best interests at heart. The NEA has made our kids a social experiment. YOU pay for the schools. YOU pay the teacher's salaries. You have a RIGHT and a holy OBLIGATION to be involved and informed about every detail of your child's education. And be courageous enough to take it to the mat if need be, knowing that many educators merely consider you uneducated and ignorant and irrelevant to your child's education.

5. A Return to Evangelism.

When I first became a Christian, the importance of telling others about Jesus was a given. You shared Him at work, at schools, at social functions, in the streets.

Now we've left that to a few evangelist, largely restricting our sharing to an occasional invitation to church. I am sure this is not what Jesus intended when he said, "Go into all the world and preach the Gospel to every creature." Never has there been a more crucial time to teach others to SHARE Jesus, for only when people come into the Kingdom can true change occur both individually and socially. For the last two decades, Satan has succeeded in making most Christians into quiet, compliant little sheep who "keep their religion to themselves." Satan fears greatly the spread of Jesus' truth. I pray for a return to the evangelistic imperative given to every believer and that once more, the righteous will be bold as a lion.

Time is getting short; now is the time for a renewal of the holy fear of repentance, the eminent place of the powerful Word of God, and to cry for a fiery, furious fresh Word from Heaven.

Now is the time to use any and all tools to equip this generation, so that when the storm hits, they will stand like steel.

24 THE GOSPEL OF VAGUE

"What I have written, I have written."

These words were spoken by Pontius Pilate. He was not a good man, and yet these words have begun to burn in me because he, at that moment, showed a quality of integrity I find increasingly absent in the modern evangelical church: The guts to stand by what you have said, and not dilute or change it because of pressure, or because it offends, or because it is expedient.

Increasingly, the modern church has become a fast-food restaurant, where its purpose seems to be to cater to the wants, whims and sensual desires of the believers. The priority is to create a church that mimics every day life so closely that one hardly knows they are at church.

It is sad to me to see what drew people to Jesus and the early church in contrast to today. People were drawn because of:

- The power of God
- Miracles
- Plain, and often cutting, truth
- The urgency of the message
- The authority of those who preached
- The call to abandon all for Him

The modern world is drawn because of:

- Gimmicks
- Self-help programs
- Media, movies and more!
- Convenience of the message
- Not having to change to belong

It has become, as my pastor pointed out last week, the Gospel of Me.

But more alarming, it has become the Gospel of Vague.

We like it when pastors preach on marriage tips, finding your purpose and keeping your chin up. Frankly, we're being comforted to death.

But when the pastor confronts gossip, or sexual impurity, or challenges people to DO something, you can feel the discomfort, even anger. As an old Pentecostal church member once said, "Preacher, now you've gone off preachin' and gone to meddlin!" And megachurches don't get built that way.

This became very clear to me recently when a youth pastor gave a message about television shows. He made it clear that he wasn't telling the kids what to watch, but just presenting the facts about the violent, occult and sexual content of their favorite shows, and challenging them to make a godly decision based on that knowledge. The rage was PALPABLE. Snide comments and ridicule followed the message. But not before we ended in worship, and I cringed as I watched the same kids who hated being challenged raising their hands in "worship".

To be fair, many of them had never been challenged on this, some grew up in unbelieving homes, and many came from Christian homes where NO ONE dared challenge the parents on their viewing habits. They have grown up seeing that their parents, if they do go to church, leave religion at the door at 12 P.M. on Sundays.

Perhaps there's hope, we'll see. But what disturbed me was that (a) They had to be told what the problem is, and (b) they were clearly angry when they were. It was the same way the parents act when the pastor gets tough. (I use that word loosely – to many, even saying, "Well, the Bible is clear about X issue" is too "tough".)

I'm thankful I cut my teeth on messages and teachers and pastors who were clear and concise on truth. It saved my life.

And what disturbs me most is not just that people are jarred and startled and angered by simple truth…

…but that there seems to be an almost complete absence of Holy Spirit conscience and conviction about these things.

The biggest reason is an absence of the truth of the Word of God in a person's life. "Thy Word have I hid in my heart that I might not sin against thee." (Psalm 119) A Holy Spirit conscience about right and wrong can only be developed if one knows what the Word of God says about something. If that is absent, there's no clear guide.

But it does not stop there. The Word of God develops in us a sensitivity to HIM. It then goes beyond a knowing that "I shouldn't watch this because the Bible says it's wrong". Your conscience is PRICKED if you watch or listen to or do something wrong! When Peter preached at Pentecost, it says they were PRICKED TO THE HEART and said, "What must we do?" What a contrast to a generation who when they are told the truth scream, "Don't TELL me what to do!" I briefly watched part of an action movie the other night that suddenly switched to the beginning of a sex encounter, and I FELT HIS PAIN and TURNED IT OFF! That's the Holy Spirit.

My grief is that this generation, and many Christians as well, does not HAVE any sensitivity to the Holy Spirit. The scriptures warn of having "their consciences seared with a hot iron." (1 Tim. 4:2) We have so much scar tissue on our hearts that nothing offends, nothing makes us ashamed, nothing makes us sorry.

And we cannot deal with even that before we deal with the real issue – the absence of clear, life-jarring TRUTH.

Most people are so media addicted that it truly is a god, an idol. An idol is anything that has taken the place in time and importance over God.

A test: Go without reading the Bible one day. What do you feel? A vague uneasiness, or nothing.

Now go without TV, computer, video games and computer for one day. What do you feel? Lost. Shaky. EMPTY. Right? Face it – you're addicted.

But worse, as this generation (and their parents) has fed the addiction, it has numbed the conscience, drowned out the voice of the Holy Spirit and filled its mind with filth, corruption, perversion and lies.

And this is a god who resents anyone challenging its central place in our lives. You only understand the spiritual nature and stronghold of this god when you point out its sin and then, look out. Pleasant people suddenly become defensive, attacking and even hateful. Doesn't that say something? If someone says, "The Bible is a lie" most believers will make a lame attempt to defend it, then walk away humiliated and defeated and feeling sorry for themselves. But ask a Christian, "Why are you reading Harry Potter, when God condemns witchcraft?" and suddenly these same believers become aggressive defenders of their own private god. That says it ALL.

But going back to the root of the issue, it is the result of years of the church becoming the Gospel of Vague. We have become little more than a self-help clinic. We are a pleasant pastel painting without clear lines or a defining image. We are an abstract art piece where everyone came come and decide for THEMSELVES what it means. We are a neat, potpourri-filled home with "Footprints" art on the wall, Christian logo coffee mugs and the latest in wholesome fiction. We are Dreamsickle Christians.

The world has had two or three generations to thoroughly dilute and delete the truth and make it irrelevant to the modern world. There have been small outposts of truth-tellers challenging the lies. But the majority have seen the handwriting on the church wall, and rather than speak the truth boldly and simply and consistently, they have lowered the standard to the level of people's sensitivities and culture's norms to make the message nice, attractive, inoffensive, and VAGUE.

In a time when so many believers cannot even clearly explain what a Christian IS, how much truth have they even absorbed, and how can we even begin to address the other issues, the issues of "How then shall we live?"

I believe we have made a huge mistake by believing if we lure people in with a happy, vague, seeker-friendly message, then eventually we can start to talk about the "tougher" issues. That is FRAUD! "Come on in, it's fun, no commitment." Then, "Well, there's a CATCH…"

Being consistent and strong in our message in this day and age will not make friends, fill your wallet or grow megachurches. But God bless all those brave men and women who dare to proclaim., "What I have written, I have written", who will not change their message to satisfy or attract the masses, or compromise and "repackage" the Gospel to make it acceptable, whose message will always be, "God's Word, nothing more, nothing less, NOTHING ELSE."

That Gospel needs no embellishment. God's Word is plain, direct and decisive. Put the Gospel ON THE TABLE, UP FRONT, with no hook or hidden agenda behind the pretty package, and it will do what it always has, what no Gospel of Vague can do – CHANGE LIVES – permanently – and raise up mighty men and women of God who are fearless and free.

25 TIMING AND OBEDIENCE

There are two kinds of time according to the Scriptures. One is Chronos, which is the linear, point-A-to-point-B time we experience as humans, and mark with clocks, calendars and dates.

The other is Kairos – God's time. In very oversimplified terms, it's God's eternal invading and intersecting of our human Chronos time. (Refer to chapter 15).

As believers, the measure of our brief lives will be the obedience we gave to God, and our responses to the Kairos moments, when His eternal plans and purposes and Voice intersected and interrupted our Chronos lives. What we do in those moments determines the value of the lives we've led, and the eternal reward and destiny we will have.

Jesus, in His 3 ½ years of ministry (and really, His whole life) walked in Kairos. People were constantly trying to pull him into Chronos living and Chronos activities. "Your time is always," Jesus said. You want what you want, when you want it, how you want it. "Be our king! Show us a miracle! Prove you are the Messiah!"

When they saw a king to free them from Rome's tyranny, Jesus saw the cross that was going to free us from the tyranny of sin. When they sought a miracle to prove he was the Messiah, He said the only miracle he was going to give them was three days dead and then Resurrection life.

He only did what He saw the Father doing. And while people paved a road for Him to be king, He followed a blood-soaked trail to be crucified. Man's Chronos demanded of Jesus that their ideas of freedom from slavery under Rome be addressed. But Jesus walked ONLY in the Father's Kairos, and from the beginning, He knew it would not be the road to success, but to DEATH.

You know, it's only recently that it occurred to me that Satan was NOT pro-crucifixion. In fact, it was the devil who attempted to get Jesus to AVOID the cross by offering him kingship if he would only bow down to him…just once…come on, just a little Jesus, take the shortcut to Glory…take the easy way…

But Jesus knew that His PURPOSE was the cross. He came to DIE. And then to rise again.

That's why when Jesus was rebuked by Peter (can you imagine the audacity?) saying, "You can't go to Jerusalem to die! God forbid!" that Jesus didn't say, "You're right, of course. Thanks, Peter" but rather said, "GET BEHIND ME, SATAN!" Why? Because Satan didn't WANT Jesus to be crucified! He KNEW something bad was coming for him, because Jesus was DELIBERATELY walking toward death on the cross!

I'm not saying Satan didn't revel in Jesus' torture and suffering and death, because he IS a sadistic monster that cannot HELP but feed on pain and bloodshed – but he did so likely in spite of his dread in knowing that Jesus CHOSE the cross – and that couldn't be good news for Satan's kingdom!

"Put away the sword," Jesus said to Peter. "Don't you know I could call down 12 legions of angels, if I wanted to be rescued? But this is how the scriptures will be fulfilled!"

"Now my soul is troubled," Jesus said. "And what shall I say? 'Father, save me from this hour'? BUT FOR THIS PURPOSE I CAME TO THIS HOUR. Father, glorify Your Name." (John 12:26-28.

He came to die. That was God's plan – and nothing could deter Him. Nothing did.

My spiritual mother once gave me a beautiful picture of God's dealings. "Look at the back of a tapestry," she said. "It's all threads and knots and is not pretty and makes no sense. But turn it over. Look how beautiful it is on the other side! We're living underneath God's tapestry for our lives. Sometimes all we see is the ugly side and the things that make no sense. But HE is weaving a masterpiece of beauty in our lives, and one day, we will see it."

God's ways are higher than ours, His thoughts are higher. He sees the

END. That is why trust and faith in His timing and His ways are so important to Him. We only see our needs, the things and people around us, the things of Chronos time. He sees it ALL. Faith asks that we trust Him, for all that we do not see – in all that we do not understand. And, faith asks that we give up the need to know. We always say, "Well, it will make sense later." Sometimes, yes – sometimes, never. Not in this life, anyway. Amy Carmichael said, "The end will explain all things." In this life, we may never understand the painful weavings, the sharp needle of a suffering, the snapping of a thread of relationship through circumstance or death. But we can know that though we may NOT know in this life the "purpose" of a thing, God has promised – Romans 8:28 – that He is at work in ALL things to produce good – if we trust Him.

When difficult things come, we are taught to fight, rebuke, bind, etc. And sometimes we should. But often difficulties are God's tools to produce a greater thing. And it is HOW WE RESPOND in the difficult things that determine the value of that work of God in us.

Joshua was a young man who grew up under Moses and became one of his most valued right hand men. He served under him for many years. There may have been moments when he thought, "Moses is old. I'm watching my best years go by. I can probably lead the people as well as he does…" But rather than allow the discontent of human understanding and Chronos to motivate or even embitter him, he trusted God's Kairos, and when the time came, he was ready, and prepared, and able to do all God asked of him. Had he let discontent and lack of trust move him, he may have tried a coup and ended up in the pit with the others who tried to rebel against Moses – and God's ways and timing. He waited on God's time. He was rewarded.

Elisha must have chafed under servanthood to Elijah. He left all he had – career, family and friends, to….wash Elijah's hands. A woman's job, by the way. You KNOW he was losing man- points for that when his old friends found out! But he stayed faithful, even though this was NOT what he expected. He trusted God – and His Kairos time. And when the time came – Elisha was given a DOUBLE PORTION of Elijah's spirit, because he was faithful in the little things, even in the things that he didn't understand.

Many of us sign on with God thinking, "I'll get this, and that, and do this, and go there" and end up disappointed and hurt and even embittered because we didn't get what we wanted or expected. We should have read the fine print of discipleship. It's not an employment opportunity that we sign on for to get great benefits. It's a draft notice where we sign our lives away to His service.

Yes, there are extraordinary benefits! But it's not a negotiated contract. It's a death warrant to our flesh, our old lives.

But oh, the glory of the surrendered life of trust! HIS choices, not mine. HIS will, HIS leading, HIS plan. The blessings of that road surpass anything we could have designed for ourselves.

I was going to be a politician. God said, "You're going into MY service." I was going to enroll in a local college. God said, "You're going to Christ for the Nations in Dallas."

I was going to be world-famous evangelist.

God said, "You will serve me in dark corners, forgotten places, bloody battlefields, and will live largely in obscurity."

I was going to change the world for Jesus.

God said, "You will be used to change the hearts of lost and forgotten ones no one knows even exist."

Has my life turned out like I wanted? Not even close. Would I have it different? Not for all the treasures, fame and acclaim the world could ever give.

Sometime after one of my big dreams was shattered – I had been set up to be exposed to the largest Christian radio audience in the world, then, without explanation, dropped …

…I found myself at a middle school church camp, signed up because a tiny church in New Mexico didn't have a youth pastor and they needed someone to go with their kids…

Our cabin was the worst on the campground. Broken curfews, fights, kicked out of worship…making me wonder at first if God was punishing me for some unrepented-of sin or misdeed.

That is, until God interjected several other kids from other churches that had no room for them in their cabins, and they ended up in our cabin. And I fell in love. One had extreme asthma and I had to watch him to make sure he was ok and got his medication. One was a big kid, who, I was told, had something wrong with him – no one knew what – but if he was cornered or made fun of, he'd go violent…

…and one autistic boy of about 11 who connected with NOBODY.

One day, two kids brought Jimmy to me. "He had an 'accident', they told me, and left him with me. This poor boy had completely lost control of his bodily functions and was standing there covered and soaked in humiliation. He looked like he just had gone into another world to avoid the humiliation he was feeling – and who could blame him? I loved the kids who brought him to me and who did not shame him. I took him back to the cabin, got him to the shower, had him hand me his soiled clothes, helped him into clean clothes and sent him back to the others. I wept as I washed his dirty clothes. I felt a love and compassion for Jimmy so deep it broke my heart.

That night at worship, Jimmy came over, sat next to me, put his head in my lap and slept.

And I understood. "Inasmuch as you have done it to the least of these, my brethren, you have done it unto Me." I didn't have to be Mega Christian. And, I no longer wanted to be. I wanted THIS. To be with the least, whom to God are the princes and princesses that are to be at the head of His banqueting table.

If I had said, "I don't want to go, it's beneath my ministry gifting," think of what I would have lost. Notice I said what I would have lost, not Jimmy. Because the reality was, instead of leaving thinking, "God must love this boy a lot to send me to him from my busy anointed life," I left broken, thinking, "God must really love me and trust me to ask me to serve one of His most loved children like this."

Sometimes I think of Stephen, cut down in his adolescence by the murdering consent of Saul of Tarsus. He would not know the joys of a full life: a wife, children, career, dreams.

No, Stephen was picked to be a waiter. (Acts 6:8) But he didn't need a big ministry or a public platform; God did wonders and signs through him in his common job – one we're not trained to aspire to in modern Christian ministry. Notice how most prophecies are, "You're going to be great! You'll stand before kings! You're going to be influential and wealthy!" Not, "God called you to be a waiter, and He's going to do mighty things through your obedience in your daily job!"

Stephen trusted God's Kairos time, and His career choice! And he obeyed. And when the moment came, he gave an epic sermon – an entire 53 verse chapter – and then was killed. But friends, even Jesus stood up to see this and welcome him Home! "I see the heavens opened and the Son of Man standing at the right hand of God!" Stephen proclaimed before he was stoned. Jesus – who SITS at the right hand of God – STOOD to receive this young hero as he gave up his life.

I promise you, he did not regret his choices. What to us might seem a human tragedy, was woven into heaven's tapestry and was a glorious and eternal TRIUMPH!

I would rather labor and walk under circumstances that humanly make no sense, if I could have a STEPHEN MOMENT that would define all God has made me for – one brilliant comet streaking through the darkness of this sinful world, then gone – than to have all the earthly success in the world with no eternal definition of my life at the end.

Trust God's eternal timing. Trust His ways. Never ask, "Why?" Always ask, "What for?" Not ONE THREAD of His dealings or our circumstance will be lost or useless – every one of them is going to make a beautiful tapestry of glory that will last for eternity.

26 TO TELL THE TRUTH

In the time of division between Israel and Judah, the King of Israel called on the King of Judah to see about doing a joint invasion of Ramoth-Gilead. But Jehoshaphat, King of Judah, requested a "prophetic confirmation." So the King of Israel called in his "gaggle of prophets" to work on it. There were individual prophets back then like Elijah, and there were "gaggles" of prophets – a kind of group thing. Kings usually had the gaggles, specially picked "yes men" who only prophesied good things. Group think has always been dangerous, you know, even today. Even Jezebel had her gaggle of Baal prophets.

After the King of Judah's prophets had their say – in which they stroked his ego and gave victorious proclamations – Jehoshaphat, aware that these were really not prophets from God – said, "Isn't there a prophet of the Lord besides, that we might inquire of him?" (1 Kings 22:7) Apparently, the Baal prophets had been slaughtered, but other questionables had taken their place.

The King of Judah's response was predictable, and telling: "There is yet one man, but I hate him; for he does not prophesy good concerning me, but evil." (1 K. 22:8) Nevertheless, Micaiah the prophet was summoned. On the way, he was advised to "play nice" and say good things to the kings. But he told them, "What God tells me, that will I speak" – the true mark of a prophet.

But when he came before them, and was asked to enquire of the Lord, (I can see him waving his hand in casual Jewish dismissal) he said, 'Yes, go and prosper, for the Lord will deliver Ramoth-Gilead into your hands."

Frankly, I understand his reaction. I am at that place with people, for example, who know the truth about things like the occult but still ask, "Is Harry Potter OK?" I want to say, "Sure, go for it. Raise your kids on it.

What God says is irrelevant, right?" But I digress…

The King obviously knew he was being dismissed and chided him to TELL THE TRUTH.

So he got it. The prophet prophesied failure and defeat. The King's response? "Didn't I tell you? He ALWAYS prophesies evil about me!" Then the King got more than he bargained for, when the prophet told of a "lying spirit" that was sent to speak through the other prophets. I should tell my Charismatic friends not to build a doctrine about "lying spirits" out of this – likely this was a "Drash" or a parable used to make a point.

The prophet was punished, the king disobeyed, and died.

Our nation is deceived. The proof: Botox. Over everyone, everywhere, looms a certainty; we will all die. And we spend our lives running from it, trying to cheat it, deceive ourselves into thinking it will not come, or we can delay it indefinitely. Youth alone matters in our culture, actual or artificial. Drug companies make billions on fear, shoving must-have fountain of youth drugs in our faces during prime time every night. Viagra is the Holy Grail of an impotent culture terrified of its own powerlessness…and of death. The media is the world's gaggle of false prophets saying, "Look and feel years younger! You have the power of CHOICE!"

But, the church needs this message about truth even more. We may be saved, but it takes a lifetime to get un-deceived, and stay that way. Most of New Testament warnings about deception are for BELIEVERS. If not at risk, why so many?

Tell Us What We Want To Hear

Most Christian media is based not on truth but on what people like to hear. And so much of it is so irrelevant. People flock to positive, self-enhancing, lifestyle-centered stuff. Prophetic conferences are filled with gaggles that are eager to prophesy, "You will succeed and prosper! God will give you a position of great power and influence!"

There remain precious few truth tellers who have not taken the church's pulse to find out what they like to eat and then give it to them, but have taken the church's TEMPERATURE to diagnose her illness and come in with a prescription from GOD. And you don't see them much on TV or with full page ads in Christian magazines or invited to crusades to speak. Why? "I hate him. He NEVER says anything positive to me!" So, the western church has been given a full gaggle of prophets to tell them exactly what they want to hear.

Truth In Fellowship

One place where we sorely need truth is in relationships in church. This is so hard for us – to learn how to speak the truth in love, not just killing each other with gossip and hate on one extreme, or loving each other into deception on the other. Christian fellowship can be so treacherous. We are one person Sunday morning and another when we leave. We bless the pastor to his face and eat him up over lunch an hour later. We have a problem with someone, and it's "off with their heads".

The King in this story is like all of us: we want God's approval, but we don't want to be told the truth about ourselves.

Church splits are most often caused by people with unexamined hearts taking a small offense, nurturing it and creating a monster. If only we could learn to deal honestly with our hurts and offences, and quickly. Unfortunately, that requires we let God – and sometimes others – tell us the truth. And then we either break, and weep, and go and mend things, or we become the King in this story: "I hate that guy. He never tells me what I like!" This is why the proverbs say, "The kisses of the enemy are deceitful; but faithful are the wounds of a friend."

But the key to this is to see our own capacity for self-defensiveness, blind-sightedness and pride. We turn a small offense into a righteous cause, tell our friends how wronged we were, and build our strategy for defending our position. And how sad, because if we allowed God to tell us the truth about our own hearts, a lot of division and strife would dry up and die. When there is an offence, our FIRST response should be Psalm 139: "Search ME, o God." God's first concern is not if you were right or wrong about your offense. It is always about YOU keeping a pure, humble and loving heart, no matter what the offense. We need God to render powerless our "righteous position." When I tend to feel justified and right about my own hurt or offense, I remember a man who wrote once, "If those who criticized me knew how much worse and more sinful a person I really was, they would have far more reason for their criticism." That is a self-examined heart. No matter how right I feel, I know that GOD knows the depraved and selfish heart that resides in me without Jesus, my own sins and failings. How can I ever feel "justified"? It's humble time.

Isn't it disturbing that Jesus said when you bring your gift to the altar, and remember that someone has something against YOU, you should drop everything and go fix it? Shouldn't it be up to the OFFENDER to fix it? I mean, they have something against ME - why should I have to fix it? But unity is precious to God. And we must do what we can to fix it even if we are right. You know. Love is ALWAYS having to say "I'm sorry!" When you get past the little god of what you "deserve" or "don't deserve", you can get to the heart of what matters to God, and in terms of broken relationships among us, hurt, offenses and church division, very little matters except healing the matter.

Frankly we aren't very good individually or corporately at honesty in these things. For example, if a pastor or youth pastor is caught in sin, or slaughtered in a bloodbath of a board meeting, their sudden absence on Sunday is explained like this from the pulpit: "The Lord has moved brother Jones on" or, "Brother Frank felt led by God into another ministry." (Yes – witnessing in the unemployment line!) It is terribly dishonest, and terribly hurtful. The people who loved them need more than a cover-up sleight of hand. Truth may be more painful but if rightly handled with healing in mind, it beats the sense of non-permanence and non-caring abandonment so often seen in church ministry.

I've seen and been through a lot of heartache over broken relationships over the years. It has always taken my breath away how quickly swords are drawn and sides are taken, and how quickly the "enemy" ceases to matter, ceases to exist. For goodness sakes, folks; Even David, whom Saul sought to kill, loved him so much he could only speak of that love, even when his life was at stake. With us, so quickly, once precious fellowship is burned on the ash heap of church politics or real or imagined hurts. You get the sense sometimes that people are just cogs in the machine of church life, and when they break down or become a problem, we just REPLACE them. Is that really fellowship? Absolutely not! But it takes a whole lot of humility, and a whole lot of pride pulverizing, to realize that whatever issues we may have are not worth sacrificing others over. But until we are willing to let God show us the TRUTH about the prideful condition of our own hearts, we will not make that bridge back to the ones we are estranged from.

I learned a different way. Years ago, my friends and I met and prayed with a lady who had been a hard core sinner and singer in Las Vegas, marvelously saved, as they say. We all bonded. She was my big sister and I was, according to her, her "father and teacher" even though we were 15 years apart!

She became ill. I moved to where she lived to become her attendant because she was almost completely disabled for a time. And we fought horribly and loudly. I was a "spoiled brat." She was "demanding and selfish." She fired me. I was right, she was wrong. (Reverse that from her perspective.) We split in anger.

We both seethed, then we remembered, and we wept. We knew that this separation from what was once pure, godly fellowship was WRONG. I asked God to reveal the truth to MY heart. And…he showed me, I was a spoiled brat. And I asked God to forgive me…and suddenly, I barely remembered what the offense was! I just longed to have my sister back…

And my friend prayed, and God showed her she was…demanding and selfish. And she repented, and called me. We met, both defensive, afraid…and reached for each other's hands across the table, and cried like babies. Love was restored. And our hearts were made whole.

How it grieves me that we do not have that in fellowship much anymore. The kind of love that, in the case of my high school "blood brother", my David's Jonathan, we disagreed, fought horribly. Accused each other. Bled. For months. Until he came to my house weeping. And I wept and we healed the wound, not CARING what the issue was. Why don't we have that, friends?

The deception is almost always that the offences are important enough to build a crusade around, one in which we build the wall high enough around our hearts that we cannot even see the one we loved, but only an "enemy." Truth about our own heart alone can shatter that, bring us into utter broken humility, and lets us hurt over the loss of precious fellowship. "Let brotherly love continue." That's the heart of the matter.

In terms of the Scripture, truth CANNOT be compromised for unity. But I have RARELY found broken fellowship or church splits to be the product of deception and people having to leave – though it seems to be happening more these days – but it is more often because of unresolved issues of the heart, caused by hurt, competition, disagreement, misunderstanding. Let God destroy our prideful position of unbending rightness, of hiding behind our anger and calling it "Holy anger" or "righteous indignation", of letting our bitterness turn our loved brothers and sisters into "the enemy." Let God speak truth TO you, ABOUT you, and go, and mend the wound. Then and only then will we understand what it is to "love one another with a pure heart fervently."

27 YOUTH MINISTRY: A CALL TO GENERATIONS

I think most of what we call youth ministry is a pretty distinctly western idea. I think it can work well, and I think it can work badly. I think we need to rethink it.

First of all, I don't think in our present culture that we're going to change the structure of youth ministry. Some elements of it are good, considering that overwhelmingly, if people aren't brought to Jesus before they are nineteen, they never come to Jesus. That's a scary thought. So I am all for major investment in youth ministry and outreach.

What I am not for is the template of youth ministry being little more than religious babysitting. I am not sure where it began, but the "sectioning off" of kids, while good for focusing teaching at a level they can grasp, has the added element of "getting them out of their parents' hair" a few times a week. Definitely not a negative for parents.

However, youth ministry is by and large considered a lesser ministry, is notoriously underfunded, and youth pastor positions badly underpaid. That in itself tells me that most people consider it not a huge priority, and youth pastors are generally treated like Junior Pastors – "Pastor Lite." And if there were ever a time when youth outreach needs to be a priority and youth pastors prayed for and supported, it is now. We send our youngest and brightest into battle in the world, knowing they are able and their role in the military is essential to everything else. Why do we not give youth pastors the same support and backing? Frankly, many churches, while paying top dollar for adult pastors, would be happy to pay just a stipend or nothing at all to get someone to handle the kids, if they can get away with that arrangement. Does that seem right to you, does that seem like we think our youth are very important at all?

There is another issue not often addressed in our current youth ministry template: What happens when a kid is no longer a kid?

I have noticed a painful reality over the years, that once a young person reaches, say, 18 to 21, they are gently nudged away from the "youth nest" of fun activities, belonging and significance into "real church." And the real world. College and career lie ahead, and likely marriage and family, and all of that is terrifying enough, but in addition, they have to deal with the loss of friends and that place they could call their own. It's terrifying, lonely and sad.

I believe it is here that we lose kids en masse. We set them adrift, without a plan spiritually or a purpose. We just expect them to grow up and adjust. After all, didn't we? (Or did we just give up all sense of spiritual purpose for a worldly pursuit of "the good life"?) But they feel abandoned. Worse, they cease to be very important to the youth pastor because they are no longer a kid. And that's the most painful of all. It's not the youth pastor's fault, it's in the nature of how we've segregated youth as a time-bound project that has an expiration date on its significance and influence. The Kingdom of God was not meant to be so divided – adults to the left, youth over to the right…we have lost the vital connection of explosive power that runs through the entire scriptures.

I believe we have left out an eternal principle that is Biblical, practical and life changing – a principle that can be the bridge to secure and further the destinies of our youth. It is the principle of spiritual inheritance and heritage.

The scriptures are clear about the command to "teach your children." The Word of God was first taught parent to child, orally, at meals, before bed, working in the fields. It was the INFUSED WORD. Infusion is the key. It wasn't just handing someone a book and saying, "here, read this." It was as intimate as Elisha laying across the dead child and literally breathing life into him.

The "mentoring" concept captures a little of this, but not nearly enough. Some have caught the idea of mentoring and "accountability" but it's much more. It is not just meeting weekly, going over a few verses and saying, "So, how's your walk with God?" It's committing to raising spiritual children, infusing God's life into them through prayer, love, the Word, example, play, work, wrestling with life, and mostly, TIME.

Elijah picked Elisha. Elisha burned his plow and followed him to learn, to "wash his hands" (a woman's job, by the way). By all Elijah said and did, he raised Elijah to one day "take his mantle" and carry God's anointing beyond his own life and time into the next generation. That was true infusion – true discipleship.

I am struck by a passage that I believe speaks to the days ahead and the need for this bridge between generations to be crossed before the final battle comes:

"Suddenly a prophet approached Ahab King of Israel, saying, 'Thus says the Lord, Have you seen this great multitude? Behold, I will deliver it into your hand today, and you shall know that I am the Lord.' So Ahab said, 'By whom?' And He said, 'By the young leaders of the provinces.' Then he said, 'Who will set the battle in order?' And He answered, 'You.'" (I Kings 20:13-14)

Do you see the model I am speaking of? Old warriors and new youth leaders had no disconnect here. One was to set up the battle, show them what to do, and the young were to carry it out. Instead we have an army of adults who just want to do adult things, and kids who are just taught to have fun and learn a few things about God.

I'm no good at discipling. I wouldn't have a clue how to schedule a discipleship moment. I do know how to pray, and how to tell stories and how to set the battle in order.

What I am today did not come as a result of merely study, experience and opportunity. Far from it. Nor did it come from sterile mentoring from men of God who were saddled with me because they had to be. No, God had chosen for me a succession of spiritual parents that infused me with life, and life-giving cornerstones that would become the foundation of who I am in God.

An 86 year old never-married Baptist lady gave me God's love and security in Him. A 50 something Christian man, by prayer and persistency, was the door that led me to the Place I found Jesus, and infused me with a love for kids who felt unloved. A young dynamic house leader infused me with the necessity and tools of evangelism, and an unswerving loyalty to God's Word. A giant of a man in Bible School taught me God's gentleness and faithfulness. A pastor-prophet from half a country away took me in as his own spiritually and taught me, by word and deed, by message and personal time with him, both prophetic truth and the human side of leadership. Two women from a city no one outside of Texas has heard of, infused me with tears, intercession, ministry principles and the longing for the deepest mysteries of adventure and intimacy with God. At every step I was infused with a richness and heritage that touches everything I now do. They, each of them, set the battle in order for me.

The spiritual bridge between generations has been almost completely washed out in the church. The message we give kids is, "Get excited about God!". The message after they are no longer a kid is, "Get a good job, marry, have kids, go to church." That's why we're losing college kids in multitudes. We start them on God's love and purpose for them, then shove them into the world, effectively castrating their purpose. Who has a plan for the long distance run? Who understands that church is not about maintaining a safe harmless life, but about a life and death battle of the ages against evil and to redeem the lost? Only then can the plan God gave to Ahab make sense. Like Ahab, those of us who are older and trained are to "set the battle in order" – explain the life goals of spiritual purpose, plan attacks against darkness, instill courage and determination, INFUSE the young with a LIFE-LONG mission in God!

And the "young leaders" are to go to war. It couldn't be clearer. The baton must be passed from hand to hand or we get a lost generation who "do not know battle."

Two things are needed for this "infusion of purpose" to happen:

1. We need men and women of God whose heart is willing to be the Elijahs who bring the young into the "school of the prophets", the Elishas who will take the young and breathe their life, love and experience into them, the Pauls who will be bold enough to say, "Follow me as I follow Christ" and thus raise up sons and daughters in the faith.

2. We need youth who want more than a purposeless, worldly purpose who will seek after their Elijahs, who will through the years beyond "youth

group" say, "Do not make me turn back. I will not! I want everything God gave you and more!"

Together, the older will set the battle in order and the young leaders will carry out the war firsthand. I may not see it in my day, but I pray for it every day. Already in some I know who are barely 20, I see it being birthed in them as they take the charge and say, "I can do that", going on missions, volunteering to minister to the younger and even youngest. Why not? I myself at 17 took the immeasurable love and gifts given me by a spiritual parent SEVENTY YEARS my elder, turned back, grabbed hold of a young life four years younger and infused God's life and purpose into them. I have never stopped, though I am now 33 years older than I was then. And every life God blessed me to infuse with His life is in my life still.

This way of ministry shatters the illusion that only young, hip people can reach youth, or that the young can only relate to someone young, or that the older kids and older adults should just go out to pasture and sit in a pew. It shatters the lie that only after years of school and preparation can a youth be a minister. They are ministers and soldiers NOW if we take hold of them and infuse them with God's lifelong purpose and gifts to them NOW. This is my burden. This is my vision.

Though we do not see the battle now, the day is soon upon us when the war will be fierce and clear, and it will be a time of "all hands on deck." Let's train the troops now and not be caught a spiritual nation with no army to fight the battle.

28 WHAT IS A CHRISTIAN?

As the years have gone by since I came to Jesus and surrendered my life to Him, I have been concerned because a lot of people, even in church, do not really know what a Christian is, or worse, THINK they are Christians when they are not. So let's go over a few basics.

First, being a good person doesn't make you a Christian. Often you can tell those who have that idea by the way they talk: Instead of "I'm a Christian", they say, "I'm Christian", or "That's not very Christian." It's not about good behavior or being a good person. Separation from God is a terminal illness with only one cure, and being a good person isn't that cure. I know many, many good people who died of terminal illnesses. One has nothing to do with the other.

So it is with separation from God. Good works and good intentions don't count if you are terminated from God because of sin. The ONLY cure is complete surrender to Jesus and receiving a new life, eternal life from Him. Put another way, you can't get to heaven by good works any more than you can get to the North Pole by driving around and around the equator. YOU CAN'T GET THERE going that direction!

Being a Christian, next, is not about trying to be one. A tree doesn't "try" to be a tree, it just is one. And a rock can't be a tree no matter how hard it tries. A tree is a tree by nature; a rock is a rock by nature. A rock can try to grow fruit, but it can't. It is by nature a rock. In order to be a Christian, you have to undergo a complete EXCHANGE OF NATURE. The rock must become a tree. An unbeliever must become a believer.

If you are not regenerated by the life of Jesus given at the cross, you can try to imitate the life of a Christian, but it is only an imitation.

I know some of this may seem very basic, but bear with me, and BELIEVE me, it's important. If you get the first button wrong when buttoning your shirt, the whole thing is off from there.

Third – going to church does not make you a Christian.

Do you remember the grade school science project where you put a celery stick in blue water overnight, and the next day the leaves have turned blue? It's called "osmosis." You can't stick yourself in a church and expect to absorb "Christian". Like Jesus said, you may be invited to the wedding, but if you don't have the clothes for it, you don't get in. The only way to get in is to have Jesus in your heart.

Next, being a Christian is not how you act, how you talk or what you do. IT'S NOT BEHAVIOR. Anyone can occasionally "behave" like a Christian. And a monkey can eventually type a word if you sit him at a keyboard long enough, but with no understanding of what that word means. Imitation is not enough. This probably comes as a shock to many Christians. Yes, our behavior SHOULD reflect our faith – but it is not its SOURCE or its CENTER. It's not about how we behave but WHO WE BELONG TO. We are either a slave to sin or a servant of Jesus. And how do you get a servant? YOU BUY THEM. We were born into the house of sin and slavery, all of us. But we become HIS PROPERTY when we receive His purchase of us paid in His own blood at the cross.

Do you belong to Jesus? I didn't ask if you behaved well! ARE YOU HIS? Did you ASK Him to buy you back from sin and destruction? That is the key to what a believer, a Christian, is – IT'S ABOUT OWNERSHIP!

Who owns you?

I love the story told in Victor Hugo's "Les Miserables" about how a priest, who had full right to turn in the thief Jean Valjean, after Valjean stole the priest's silver, instead told the police who had caught Valjean that he was a friend and he gave him the silver as a gift. It was the moment that changed Valjean's life forever. From there came the riveting words that would define the rest of his life: MY SOUL WAS BOUGHT FOR GOD.

Anyone who does not understand the price of purchase paid by Jesus' horrible death and spilled blood and who has not asked for redemption – purchase – is not a Christian. It's that simple.

Next, believing in the Christian philosophy does not make you a Christian. You say you believe in God, believe in Jesus, heaven and hell. That is not enough. Even the demons believe, the book of James says, and tremble with fear. And demons aren't saved.

So what does REAL belief mean? The Amplified Bible is helpful here: "Believe (trust, cling to, rely on) the Lord Jesus Christ, and you will be saved." Do you trust, cling to and rely on Jesus? THAT indicates you are saved, not just a vague belief that something about Jesus may be true. It's like the story of the stunt man at Niagra Falls who asked the crowd, "Who believes I can take a man in a wheelbarrow across this falls suspended on this high wire?" One man said, "I do." "Then", the stunt man said, "Get in the wheelbarrow." The true Christian does not talk; they are committed to the one who will take them across the cavern of death into eternity. Their belief in Jesus made them get in the barrel.

Do you really trust Jesus with your whole life that way?

Next, believing in a Christian code of ethics doesn't make you a Christian. Someone may say, "I don't believe in abortion, drugs, homosexuality, stealing, adultery", etc. But neither did the religious leaders of Jesus day. Yet Jesus told them that prostitutes would get into heaven before they did! Why? Because they had the right ideas and the right actions but not a right HEART. The worst sinner who abandoned their hearts and lives to Jesus was embraced by Him, but the "moral" people were rejected because they never gave their HEARTS to Him! And THAT is all He wants. Again, it's not ethics, it's a matter of WHO OWNS YOUR HEART! Who owns yours? If Jesus doesn't have your heart, all the good values you have mean nothing at all. Jesus said there would be people on judgment day that said, "We did good works, we did spiritual things!" And Jesus said, "Go away from me, I NEVER KNEW YOU."

Do you KNOW Him?

Being a Christian is not God fixing your old life. It is unfixable. Maybe you have asked God to fix you and make you a "better person." It's not enough.

No – you must face the fact that you were BORN WITH A TERMINAL SPIRITUAL ILLNESS – it's called the sin nature – and you can't fix or repair that. It will kill you for eternity. It is IN you, and you will die spiritually from it.

Being good won't cure you. Good ethics won't cure you. Proper beliefs won't cure you.

You must let the person you are, DIE. You must give that sinful, destructive, ugly OLD life to Jesus to be put to death, and exchange it for His life – eternal life.

Jesus said, "You must be born again." He said we are born once, of human birth. But to receive eternal life, you must be born AGAIN, born of His Spirit. The old must die; the new must come.

Being a Christian is about a complete change in identity. It is a change of species, of spiritual DNA. You were born of this world, this blood, this earthly fallen race.

When you surrender to Jesus, you are given a completely new bloodline – the Royal blood of God Himself – and you are free from the terminal blood disease of sin and given a new identity, a child of God – and a new citizenship in Heaven.

Have you been born again?

How do you BECOME a Christian?

It's so easy, as someone said, most people stumble right over it. And it won't cost you anything – just your life. You cannot buy it – it is a free gift. But you have to RECEIVE it. To be born again, you have to ask. You have to recognize you need saving, and you need Jesus to save you from sin. You must ask for Him, to surrender your all to Him.

It begins with a simple prayer. If you recognize you are not a Christian after reading this, or aren't sure, and if you are ready to surrender your all to Jesus, you can pray this simple prayer:

"God, I know I am a sinner and I can't save or fix myself. I can't be good enough to get to heaven. I need you. Jesus, I believe You died on the cross for me. My sins nailed you to the cross. Jesus, forgive me! Forgive me of my sins. I completely surrender my life to you. I lay down my old life…to die to my old life…Jesus, give me new life, YOUR life. Come into my heart, Jesus. Make me born again. My life is Yours. Make me into the person You want me to be. In Jesus' Name. Amen."

If you pray this prayer and mean it with all your heart, you need never wonder again if you are a Christian. You will know!

Now go out and change the world!

29 GREATER THINGS

"Seekest thou great things for thyself? Seek them not." (Jeremiah 45:5)

What is it to be great in God's Kingdom?

We are all victims of faulty thinking about this. As someone who has been allowed to do "big" things and small, see awesome miracles and felt the searing heat of desert winds, failure and human abandonment, I now realize I had it all wrong.

What is great to us is not to God.

What is great to God, we would not seek.

Contemporary ministry is designed to be about bigness, success, results. Isn't it? If someone set about to fulfill their calling today, this would be the goal:

- Establish a name and a 501c3.
- Get an Internet presence.
- Knock on doors.
- Pursue speaking engagements.
- Get interviewed.
- Develop a "vision plan".
- Raise funds.
- Publish a book.

Results in today's ministry are based on:

- How big is your congregation?

- How many souls have you won to Christ?

- How many programs do you have?

- How many people support you?

- What is your annual donation base?

- What size is your staff?

I have to tell you; I have failed at nearly every goal I just listed. I don't knock on doors. I've never gotten a publisher to publish my books. I have a very tiny donor base. I don't seek places to speak. By current ministry standards, I am an abject failure. In fact, by those standards, 90% of pastors and missionaries are failures.

Maybe we need to rethink success and spiritual greatness.

It was sad to read the editor of a major Christian magazine, as a preface to their article on a megachurch, chide small churches and their pastors for not having a vision, for settling for small. Believe me, many of them dream of Big but still serve in the small.

I'm not against Big, if God does it. I'm not against well-known ministers, if God does the promoting.

But neither big churches nor popular ministers means spiritual greatness. God doesn't measure that way. We have to differentiate between great things God does and spiritual greatness. God saves whom He will, moves as He pleases, redeems by the thousands or more because He wills to – and He'd do so with or without us. If He uses us, that's our blessing, not His need.

I wanted to write this because there are multitudes of Christians and servants and pastors who feel so insignificant, so tiny, even useless – partly because they compare themselves to the media idea of Big Things in Christianity. They serve in small arenas but in big ways – unnoticed, unappreciated, unthanked. They do it because they love Jesus, and they love people. And that's HUGE to God.

Twice in my life I have reached the "pinnacle". In 1978, I had a 2,000 person-mailing list, I was in demand all year, I was on the 700 Club, wrote articles for a major Christian magazine, and became chairman of a blossoming international ministry. And one day, it came crashing down. I wasn't in sin. I hadn't disobeyed.

I did not understand, until a few years later, when I was living in a tiny town called Everman, Texas, not knowing if I was even "called to ministry" anymore.

In the midst of that test of seeming failure and isolation, God drew about eight neighborhood kids into my life. They became my "ministry" for the next two years, hanging out with them, playing, bike riding, and teaching them about Jesus.

I thought my previous full schedule and prestigious position was "big ministry."

God thought eight kids were.

Then, called to El Paso in 1987, within a year, I was back on top – constant travel, vital youth ministry that saw nearly 1000 kids in ten years, appearances on Geraldo and Montel Williams, you name it. It was an important and intense time.

Then, suddenly, in 1997 during the illness and death of my dad, it all crashed and burned. I wasn't in sin. I didn't disobey. It was just…TIME.

Of course, in the midst of grief and human abandonment, I did not understand. Not until I was asked to take four kids to a dismal summer camp in New Mexico, where I was assigned to the worst and neediest kids there. I was disrespected by camp counselors half my age, moving like a phantom for five days among them.

But they brought David to me, a boy with debilitating asthma, and Frank, a big, angry hurt kid who scared the younger counselors. They became my flock, my special charge. And I had one boy who was semi-autistic. They "dumped" him on me one day because he'd had an "accident," and they didn't know how to deal with the mess. I took him and helped him clean up and change into clean clothes and go back to the group. I did it without embarrassing or shaming him. Other kids had already done that. And then I washed his clothes. I don't share this to make myself look good, far from it.

But that evening, during the worship service, when this 11 year old, who could not bond with anyone, lay his head in my lap and fell asleep, I understood. To God, this was "big" ministry. This was His HEART.

There are times I have longed for the "big stuff," I confess. It was hard to read of big Christian superstars and writers who'd written 70 books, and their latest was a million seller. It was spiritual envy, and it was a sin, and I left it behind.

But there was a deeper thing. A sense that I wish I'd done, could do more, for Jesus- for all that He had done for me.

Somewhere at the five-mile mark outside of Benson, Arizona, heading to Tucson, I was driving and prayed, "Jesus, I've done so little for You. So little!" He replied in a gentle voice that brought me to tears, "Every young life that you have loved, you loved for Me." I understood in that moment what really mattered to Him, and I've not wanted more since. Just to be His heart, letting Him love kids through me, for Him, with Him.

No, God does not measure greatness as we do. I read one day that the day JFK was assassinated, when all the world reeled in shock and sorrow, there was a small obituary buried on the back page of a British newspaper for a man named CS Lewis. Humanly, it seems unfair. JFK lived a selfish, corrupt life and was hailed as a hero in death. CS Lewis wrote books, lectured about the Christian faith and loved Jesus, and died with hardly a mention.

But oh, the welcome waiting for him on the other side!

There was a song called "Thank You" about someone going to heaven, and one person after the other coming up to say, "Thank you for giving to the Lord." He was welcomed by people he barely remembered, people he did not know, who had come to Jesus because he taught Sunday School, gave to missions.

We see only the back side of this tapestry, a tangled knot that often makes no sense, has no apparent beauty, just a seeming endless praying, serving, loving, often with no visible fruit at all.

But oh, my friend, on that Day when He turns the tapestry over, you will know just how much He did and was able to do because you gave, you loved, you obeyed!

I think of Amy Carmichael, who as a young girl left all her privilege in England for the mission field, ending up in the small village of Dunhavur, India. She spent her life rescuing children from temple prostitution. She built a home for them. She never became "famous," never saved the multitudes, built no mega ministry, and never returned to her home in England. In fact, she spent the last twenty years of her life unable to get out of bed. But she WROTE.

Her mission still stands in India. And her books, written in adversity and illness, reach across the decades and continue to touch lives for eternity, and so they have touched me.

The world – the church – would not consider her great. But GOD does.

My loved friend, God knows your heart, and your service, your giving and your love for the hurting and the lost. You too have said, "Have I really done anything for Jesus? Has my life mattered?" To you, Jesus says, "Inasmuch as you did it to the least of these, you have done it to Me. I was hungry, you fed me…naked, you clothed me…in prison, you visited me."

Do you want to know the path to true spiritual greatness? It is defined by four words, and in these four words, true ministry is eternally defined:

"Jesus took a towel." (John 13:4)

YouthFire Publications

Box 370006

El Paso TX 79937

www.gregoryreid.com

ABOUT THE AUTHOR

Gregory Reid is an ordained minister with American Evangelistic Association with an honorary doctorate from Logos Graduate School and is a retired Private Investigator. He has been a believer in Jesus since July 20th 1969, and has been in ministry since 1975. Over the years, Dr. Reid has been involved in crisis counseling, overseas missions, media ministry, youth ministry and a number of other outreaches. His primary love and commitment is to youth ministry, and is currently a youth pastor in Texas.

Made in the USA
Charleston, SC
29 August 2016